Breaking Generational Silence

Also by Nicole Russell-Wharton

Everything a Band-Aid Can't Fix

My Busy, Busy Brain

Breaking Generational Silence

A Guide to Disrupt
Unhealthy Family Patterns
and Heal Inherited Trauma

NICOLE RUSSELL-WHARTON

sounds true
BOULDER, COLORADO

Sounds True
Boulder, CO

Published 2025

Cover design by Jess Morphew
Book and jacket design by Charli Barnes

Printed in the United States of America

BK07024

Library of Congress Cataloging-in-Publication Data

Names: Russell-Wharton, Nicole, author.
Title: Breaking generational silence : a guide to disrupt unhealthy family patterns
    and heal inherited trauma / by Nicole Russell-Wharton.
Description: Boulder, CO : Sounds True, 2025. | Includes bibliographical
    references.
Identifiers: LCCN 2024027077 (print) | LCCN 2024027078 (ebook) | ISBN
    9781649632999 (trade paperback) | ISBN 9781649633002 (ebook)
Subjects: LCSH: Minority families--Psychological aspects. |
    Generational trauma. | Dysfunctional families.
Classification: LCC HQ728 .R87 2025 (print) | LCC HQ728
    (ebook) | DDC 306.87--dc23/eng/20240820
LC record available at https://lccn.loc.gov/2024027077
LC ebook record available at https://lccn.loc.gov/2024027078

FSC
www.fsc.org
MIX
Paper | Supporting
responsible forestry
FSC® C103098

This book is dedicated to my son and co-author, Cash. At the beginning of this journey, I had no idea you would join me on this ride, making me a mother and giving me even more inspiration and determination to piece together our family puzzle as you grew in my womb. My history is your history, and one day I hope you read this book with pride. From writing on the brink of exhaustion and pure adrenaline, to writing in the car as your father drove us to doctor appointments, we got it done, kid! Anything we put our minds to, we will get it done.

Contents

Introduction

To accept one's past—one's history—is not the same
thing as drowning in it; it is learning how to use it. An
invented past can never be used; it cracks and crumbles
under the pressures of life like clay in a season of drought.

—James Baldwin

If I could sit across the table and have a conversation with one of my
ancestors, I would choose Ms. Geraldine Brandt, the woman who
gave birth to my mother. I would set the table with a dish of seasoned
white beans and rice and a glass of brandy, her favorite. After telling
her how much I missed her radiant smile, I'd enthusiastically share
everything she'd missed since her passing. I'd walk her through the
many ailments that almost cut my time short and the similarities we
shared. I would tell her how her only child, my mother, both struggled and prevailed in her absence, doing the best she could for herself
and her children.

Maximizing whatever time I could buy, I would ask my grandmother
questions that stem from my own self-doubts, hoping that my openness
would inspire her to do the same. I'd seek answers to questions never
asked, not by anyone else in my family, and certainly not by me. With her
permission, I would ask about the knowledge she gained from enduring

multiple miscarriages and if she'd ever heard of conditions like endometriosis, something I imagine was inherited from her womb to mine.

No longer grandma's baby, I would sit with her, woman to woman, and gather the information I deserve to know, granting me the opportunity to face the inevitable more prepared. I would ask about my complex organs, and if this, too, was something passed down through my DNA. I'd look for guidance on how to comfort myself through my body's unpredictable setbacks, hoping she also required much of the same. I'd want to know if my grandmother also dealt with consistent health scares and mental health issues or if she had the same fears I did about keeping a man when bearing children wasn't easy. And in the gentlest words, I would ask her if she, too, felt like less of a woman due to her challenges with fertility.

Have you ever wondered what consequences have resulted from the stories never shared in our families and communities? Have you wondered what answers to familial questions have evaded us due to a lack of total truth about how we arrived at our current destination? I certainly have, and honestly, I feel more challenged and less equipped to face my future because of this lack of familial understanding. This uncertainty and misdirection are the result of what I call generational silence. In the digital age of short attention spans and constant stimulation, where we're bombarded with never-ending streams of content, the voices of our elders often fade into the background, leaving a void of knowledge in their absence. It's within our family tree and the invaluable stories passed down across generations that we understand the complex makeup of our DNA and feel prepared for what's ahead. This is why it's important that we break generational silence and refuse to perpetuate it in our lives and those of our children or younger generations.

When we break generational silence, we:

- Live in our truths rather than our beliefs or uncertainties

- Recognize that growth is no longer personal and impacts the entire family tree

- Have greater chances to heal and mend fractured relationships

- Gain insights into the rationale behind our parents' and grandparents' decisions

- Strengthen connections and resiliency within the family

- Improve the likelihood that we rest in peace when our time is up on earth

- Become better self-advocates

- Reduce generational trauma

Healing, whether mentally or physically, requires us to learn that we can never truly master self-development or grasp the root of our needs without understanding our genetic makeup. While I can work with what I know of myself, there's still so much more that I carry within me that has been left unseen and unexplored. I've spent the past two years sitting with the revelations of my body, going from surgery to surgery, trying to figure out what's solely mine and what I have inherited from those before me. I've become overwhelmed with my emotions—frustration, sadness, anger, and confusion—which have never guided me toward solutions but have, instead, led me to realize that my request for healing can only be found through an endless string of truths that have lain dormant for too long. I didn't have the privilege of long, deep familial conversations growing up, and the ones I did have were very surface level. They never provided the information I needed to prepare me for the health battles and life circumstances I'd encounter one day.

At thirty-seven, I've learned that my questions won't always yield definitive answers, but greater understanding can bring solace. It wasn't until I started inquiring about my genetic identity that I had the awakening that generations of insecurities were nurtured by fear and a lack of support. These occurrences eventually led my people to hold their truths as secrets, keeping both moments of pain and revelation to themselves. I see these issues not just in my family but in the many families of the children I work with in disadvantaged and perpetually overlooked communities. But there are relatable secrets within every family, of every class and every race.

To uncover the secrets and get to the other side, I needed to address my healing challenges, all of which are rooted in my family's silence, psychological pathology, and the imprint that slavery left on both sides. This is the journey this book will kick-start for you as well.

Silence Is Too Common

Generational silence is a term widely used in psychology, sociology, and anthropology to describe patterns of communication and avoidance that persist across generations. It is often used when referencing families who have experienced suppressed thoughts or repressed emotions about a common issue for at least two generations. Generational silence resonates across all communities, but its weight is particularly profound within families whose histories are intertwined with trauma, which encompasses not only their physical and mental health but also their struggle for justice and equality. Although the stories of previous generations remain buried in the past, allowing us to avoid the risk of endangering our well-being, the pain they unjustly endured molds the foundations of new generations.

Physically dismantling these patterns of repeated suppression in an attempt to holistically help oneself is no easy feat, and our efforts can manifest themselves in many ways, including demanding respect and fair compensation, equitable employment opportunities, preventative health screenings, and the resources required to discover our ancestral truths. This work also often involves taking complex steps like openly sharing the intricacies around the sorrows that built emotional walls between us and the pains that keep our soul ties at a distance.

I believe that every individual's commitment to healing positively impacts the world. It's the type of healing that shakes the fruit off a tree and feeds communities and families. And so the thought that we're here to just fulfill a purpose, a singular task, pales in comparison to the greater task of challenging the silence that plagued those who brought us here, helping us live beyond limited understanding and form new realities for ourselves. When we become complacent among the silenced, we end up living a life directed by a misguided self-perception and lessen our ability to meet our greatest potential. Finding a solution to personal problems, making informed decisions, or realizing our full potential depends on our capacity to grasp as much available information as possible from both our ancestral and personal pasts. It requires us to collect family data and learn as much as we possibly can about where we come from. These genetic ties hold the key to our deepest beliefs, perceptions, and fears, and taking the time to understand these hidden aspects of ourselves can open the door to a higher level of self-awareness and personal accountability.

How many of us really know and understand the contents of our DNA and the trauma we carry from experiences that are not our own? Have you ever had the privilege of talking to your mother about the daily stressors she faced while carrying you in her womb or the intrusive thoughts she carried postpartum? It's also important to note that ancestral memory extends beyond the confines of our familial narratives. It proposes that memories, experiences, and traits from our ancestors influence their descendants' behavior, perceptions, and physical characteristics across generations. Though not scientifically proven, some researchers suggest that epigenetic mechanisms—epigenetics is the study of heritable and stable changes in gene expression that occur through cultural transmission—may contribute to this phenomenon, implying that aspects of our ancestors' lives and experiences persist within us, shaping our identities and impacting how we engage with the world.

Through my nonprofit organization Precious Dreams Foundation, I work with children in the foster care system and those who are unhoused. Since our inception, we've created local chapters across the states and served over 25,000 youth. In NYC, we are part of the first responding teams that welcome youth into care and help them navigate the transition from these systems, offering them support and necessary tools through our first-of-its-kind, brick-and-mortar Comfort Shop, self-soothing workshops, and mental health programs. About 94 percent of the youth we serve are children of color who often ask me questions like "Why did my parents give up on me?" "Was I not good enough?" or "Why me?" I know the answers they so desperately seek will never be received unless their families are healed enough to give honest responses.

Even the most present parents will tell you they did the best they could with what they were given. But I believe it's only the most healed parents, the ones who are brave enough to face unfavorable judgment, who will admit to their shortcomings and understand how their own upbringing and life circumstances influenced their decisions or mistakes and, by extension, their parenting. By facing their truths, these parents have the power to profoundly impact and potentially save their children from unnecessary years of confusion and pain.

For youth seeking to understand their place in the world, this loss of familial connectedness can result in feeling a lack of belonging altogether. This thought alone often leads me to think about the many migrant youth in the US who were sent away from their home countries to hopefully find safety and opportunity in a new land. Psychologists Marshall Duke and Robyn Fivush conducted a study at Emory University that suggested that having an "intergenerational self" or family narrative boosted children's self-esteem. Asking children a simple series of questions like "Do you know where your mom and dad went to school?" "Do you know an illness or something really terrible that happened in your family?" and "Do you know the story of your birth?" helped inform the psychologists' conclusion that the more children knew about their family histories, the more control they felt over their lives and the more they believed their families functioned successfully. Understanding that children with a stronger sense of family narrative typically have feelings of control over their lives and higher levels of emotional well-being, it's easier for me to understand why the kids at Precious Dreams Foundation have a harder time perceiving their ability to overcome challenges. Despite their immense capabilities, they are held back, in part, by the undisclosed circumstances and secrets that they were born into.

Creating this book has become a journey of healing for everyone involved—the children I work with, my family, friends, agent, book coach, therapist, and editor. As I continue to nurture these relationships, both new and old, I've learned that generational silence is a shared experience among us all. During one of my 6:00 am writing sessions, I received an email from my literary agent that said, "The day after my dad was diagnosed with cancer, I found out my biopsy came back positive for melanoma. That, plus a family history of cancer (my mom and her mom both had cancer in their forties), has inspired me to see a cancer genetics counselor, especially as I look to start a family of my own. I've thought of your project the entire way through this journey and have encouraged my siblings to explore the same testing. There hasn't been much I can control, but I can control this, and it's given me a pathway toward healing in its own way."

Once complete strangers, I found myself sharing things with my writing team that I've never shared with my therapist, and vice versa. The weight of responsibility I felt from those keeping me account-able made it even harder to write and, at times, inspired insecurities that led to self-defeating thoughts. Nevertheless, penning this book was a mission I felt compelled to fulfill. I had the revelation to write this book in 2022 while taking my first solo shower after a string of surgeries that left me with nerve damage on the entire right side of my upper body and, thus, partly immobilized. I knew that writing, as it had done countless times before, could save my life as I continued to search for answers. I needed to document the process of mentally and physically healing while learning my new body and find a way to keep my discoveries in a place that could be found one day to hopefully help someone else.

My heritage as a descendant of the Russell and Medina family tree is a mix of Black, Latin, and European descent. Growing up on Long Island, I used to explain that in full to people whenever they asked about my race. Naïve, I felt it benefited me to explain to others that I was like them in some way, overexplaining for acceptance. Now as an adult, I simply identify as Black because, at the end of the day, that is how I'm seen by the world, regardless of my genetic makeup.

My father's lineage traces back to a small town named Estill in South Carolina, where today's population consists of just under 2,000 people. Like most Black families, our history is intertwined with the complexity of the United States's deep-rooted racial issues. On one hand, my family grew up on the "Russell Plantation," and on the other, I was recently able to trace my maternal grandparents' whereabouts back to New York City, but that's as far as I've been able to go. There's so much history lost, similar to many others. Being of Puerto Rican, Black, and Mexican descent, my mother takes great pride in her heritage, though she never had the chance to learn about her culture or history firsthand, never visiting her ancestral homeland or learning the language.

The interconnected stories of my ancestors remained unexplored until I began writing this book. Learning so much each day through conversation and online research, I started to discover just how many missing pieces existed in my puzzle. Why didn't my parents ask their parents personal questions? Were they told not to? Why didn't they choose to share their childhood challenges or the traumatic experiences that shaped them into the people I now call Mom and Dad? And now that I was beginning to initiate these conversations, how could I expect my parents to understand the power of their voice, especially if no one had shown them the importance of it? After all, they're Black Americans. And for Black people in the United States, recognizing and utilizing one's voice for progress is still strangely celebrated as a unique occurrence rather than a standard practice. In many ways, writing this book feels like an act of resistance as I intentionally turn the lights on in a metaphorically dark and dusty room and go against the behavioral strategies that were passed down within my family. My research thus far has revealed another example of how the oppressor has yet to be held accountable for the immeasurable impact of systemic inequities that have kept my family quiet for decades, if not centuries.

As I came to understand where this silence stems from, I had to ask myself an important question: If my parents barely speak to me about the past, how can I convince them to allow me to share their past with the world through my work? In setting myself up for this challenging journey, I'm bound to ruffle some feathers and make others uneasy, but that's not my intention; I simply seek truth, which is the one thing that has the power to set us all free. I had to lean on faith that my family would understand that.

I often think about how many Black people carry so much pride in their culture and family traditions despite the harsh realities and adversities we face. To do this, all while living in a society that hasn't shown any interest in our familial security, feels like pure bravery. In the modern day, family separation—particularly within the foster care system—disproportionately affects Black and Brown families. In fact, African American families are overrepresented in reports of suspected maltreatment and are subjected to child protective services (CPS) investigations at higher rates than other families.[1] This historical trend of family separation and the disinterest in keeping Black families together can be traced back to the forced sale of men, women, and children during slavery.

In her book *Help Me to Find My People*, Heather Andrea Williams uses personal narratives of enslaved people, historical documents, and public records to explain the heartbreak caused by forced family separation. Desperate for reunification, mothers would walk from plantation to plantation in search of their children, and families would take out "Information Wanted" ads in hopes of finding their kin. She explains, "Sources offer clear evidence of deep pain on the part of those who lost family members and they also suggest that the expression of this pain in the presence of whites was sometimes muted, silenced, or buried, because whites would not tolerate it and perhaps also because blacks thought that expressing their grief openly would avail them of nothing."[2] Heather shines a light on the undying hope and unwavering determination of Black Americans to survive and thrive in their pursuit of family and connection, despite the gaps our history has left along the way.

Piecing my family's story together took great effort and mental stamina. Reflecting on their silence forced me to think about my ancestors' sacrifices, their limited beliefs, and the ways in which they were forced to conform in order to be accepted by the outer world. I've thought about them being forced to adhere to the oppressive realities of the time, stripped of the ability to enact any form of lasting change. This led me to dive deeper into their stories, exploring the many ways conformity came at the cost of their overall health—mental, physical, and spiritual.

My paternal great-grandmother was raised on a plantation that once housed slaves. She, by all accounts, was a white-presenting woman who disapproved of her rebellious children, who all married brown-skinned people and had melanated grandchildren. If your skin was dark enough that someone could tell you were "colored," you were unwelcome in her home, regardless of your relation to her. The trauma she must have experienced to adopt this thought process and reject her family, the harm she internalized and later passed down, and the ideas of unworthiness she must have felt rattle my spirit even in mere contemplation. It leaves me frustrated, knowing that it wasn't just a choice but a sacrifice that my pale-skinned grandfather made in marrying a dark-skinned Black woman. In choosing to move North, he sacrificed everything so he could provide a better life for his children and their future children, including me.

No matter where or who you come from, there are secrets in your family, and those secrets hold the key to unlocking generational patterns of both thought and action. Even if you are estranged from your family, adopted, or completely detached from your biological lineage, you carry DNA that you can learn about through conversations with those who may have known your loved ones, online research, and/or public files. Don't question whether it's worth knowing the truth. After processing the emotions that come with the truth, you'll find that truth is the reality that propels your spirit into a place of healing, not only for yourself but others. In each part of this book, you'll be met with questions that can help you spark these conversations, as well as tips to support you in diving beneath the surface to piece together a family narrative with the actions, successes, and failures of those who have come before you.

I share my path toward discovering my family history and documenting their stories, and I hope to inspire you to reflect on your personal journey and the topics your family has opted to leave unexplored. Throughout the book we will discuss many of these taboos, like financial literacy, religion, violence, health challenges, relationship struggles, and overall self-confidence. While there's no one-size-fits-all formula for healing, I believe learning as much as possible about the genes you carry within you can serve as an advantage. I hope each chapter sparks more curiosity, courage, and important conversations for you—for your family and those across generations.

> "I don't know how you heal a wound
> and not let it get some air."
>
> —Barbara Neely

Acknowledging our traumas is critical in truly moving forward and creating sustainable change. Becoming familiar with our families' narratives is necessary if we want to enrich our understanding of self, including our genetic disposition, to recalibrate our journey toward healing. When you break the generational silence within your family, you improve your self-advocacy skills. How many times have you been caught off guard to answer triggering questions from health professionals or communicate your emotional needs to your partner? Breaking the pattern of poor communication gives us the opportunity to create a new path forward. It allows us to address the deep issues that have held our families back in unknown ways, then heal both ourselves and our lineage.

As we dive into this work, please know that if breaking generational silence were a simple task, we would've done it centuries ago;

we would do it all the time. The journey you are about to embark on in this book will demand your highest level of determination. As you begin the work of initiating conversations, you will find that some are one-sided and certain memories may cause emotional triggers. You will certainly need a community to listen to your struggles, a journal to keep records, and perhaps even a good therapist to help you process not only your complex emotions but the discomfort that comes with asking those around you to revisit a place they once left without intending to return.

May the resilience of your ancestors guide your steps to success and bring you closer to the people you call family in a healthier way. All it takes is one family member to stand up and commit to the work that has the power to propel subsequent generations toward success. And if you're holding this book, that person is you. I hold you, dear reader, in the same admiration that I know my ancestors held me in long before I existed. If you're reading this, in many ways you're already ahead of me. You are brave and curious about finding ways to better yourself. You surpass me in courage, and I urge you to utilize this book and my words as supportive cheerleaders in propelling you toward your greater self. You got this!

Encouraging Words for Your Journey

Repeat the following encouraging words to yourself as needed or to prepare for days when you're engaging in difficult conversations.

- My determination to heal intergenerational trauma sets my elders free of their unconscious weight of unworthiness.

- I stand firm against the continuation of unhealthy generational cycles and fixed mindsets.

- I am worthy of total healing.

- The body I have inherited is strong and able.

- While I'm still learning who I am, I love what I've come to know.

- I don't run from challenges; I seek truths.

- My efforts unlock new paths that soothe the pains of my elders.

Part One

My Mother's Silence

Chapter One

Your Mother's Tears

If I have learned anything in my life, it is
that the only way to get where you want to
go is to know where you came from.

—Quincy Jones

How much do you know about the pain your mother carries?

I invite you to reflect on this question for a moment. There's something really special about asking questions, as it can lead you down a rabbit hole toward truths that completely alter your perspective about life and the reality you've created. Life changed for me the day I asked my mother about her tears. An inquisitive child, I wanted badly to understand her emotions. Now as an adult focusing inward, I've become determined to turn that childlike curiosity toward myself and understand the triggers behind my tears and the generational sorrows that may influence them. When my mother cries, I see the tears of my ancestors forming a river that flows through time. I feel centuries of pain that turned my mother's expressed emotions into an act that carries more weight than the present moment. In turn, it becomes a spiritual experience marked by the blood, sweat, tears, and energy of those who paved our way, and I don't even think she's aware of it.

Our mothers are the maps we need to find our way home—home to the messages and gems of freedom that were ingrained deep in the hearts of our ancestors for us to find. Getting to the root of who I am, as well as who my mother is, started with turning to her for answers and accepting that some of my personal challenges not only stemmed from her but from my genetics and intergenerational trauma. It has been a heavy burden to bear, the thought that we carry pain we didn't ask for. And acceptance has made all the difference, eventually bringing on a sense of relief. I know that when I choose joy, it isn't just a conscious decision but something I've worked toward.

How we respond to pain impacts more than just ourselves. Embracing that, in some way, we all carry intergenerational trauma has helped me not only live well but forgive my mother for her shortcomings. This renewed outlook has allowed me to understand that she is the product of many influences, some of which she may have never had the capacity, resources, or words to fully grasp. Intergenerational trauma, also known as transgenerational trauma, is an emotional or psychological trauma experienced by a group of people that affects the health and well-being of individuals in successive generations.[1] While it manifests differently in everyone, impacted generations will often show signs and symptoms like depersonalization, emotional numbness, depression and anxiety, blemished life skills, a lack of self-worth, and post-traumatic stress.[2] This is one of the many reasons I aim to not only heal myself but my entire bloodline: to repair the past, the present, and even the future.

"Some people cannot be cured, but everyone can heal."

—Unknown

My journey toward uncovering my family history began with a simple conversation. While direct and intimate communication with my loved ones has always been afforded to me throughout my life, I admit that I don't come from a family that often talks about healing modalities, mental health, or coping techniques in particular. We never held space to share our wellness tips or address our childhood traumas. So, as an adult, it's taken discomfort and a lot of bravery to break that cycle. Using my approach to the Precious Dreams Foundation as inspiration, I've centered my nonprofit's mission on the very themes that champion the cause of wellness each day, and while it took me some time, I'm finally at a place where I'm ready to bring that mission home.

To create lasting change, one that would have a ripple effect on future generations, I decided to speak to the woman God used as a vessel to bring me into the world. The woman responsible for my life. From a young age, I always felt that I represented the fullest realization of my mother's bravest intentions. I was empowered to be the better version of her, and that was the legacy she aimed to leave in raising me. Through her prideful eyes, I've always felt as though I had the ability to articulate the thoughts she would often shy away from speaking.

One Sunday afternoon, I called my mother and asked if she could answer some questions for me. Wasting no time, I asked, "Mom, do you think one of your parents had a mental disorder?" Her contemplative response, "That's a good question!" was followed by a long pause. It soon became evident that, while she didn't have an exact answer, she held certain suspicions. My mother had never thought to ask her own parents such a personal question. This realization struck me deeply and highlighted the contrast between my mother's openness with me and her reluctance to do the same with her own parents.

My mom confided in a pensive tone, "I never asked my parents about mental health. Growing up, my parents just didn't discuss their pasts. I could see challenges in my dad through different behavioral episodes, but I would just try to calm him down. I wouldn't ask questions. My mother was incredibly stern, so I learned early on not to question or ask too much, especially when she seemed stressed. I wanted to break that communication barrier with my own kids. I wanted you to know you could come to me about anything. Reflecting on it now,

I think she handled her stress through drinking and smoking. She was a chain-smoker. That was her form of self-medication back in the day."

Angie

My mother, Angie, is the only person in my immediate family who will stay to the end of a difficult conversation to answer all my toughest questions. Even if she only engages in these types of conversations when I initiate the dialogue, she remains present, despite her discomfort. Broadening my understanding of myself required me to educate myself on my mother's history. To do so, I began calling her more frequently to connect. My mother lives in Florida, and I reside in New York, so I only see her about once a year, but that doesn't get in the way of our calls. Sundays allow for us to spend the most time in conversation together, so we started referring to these talks as "Soul Sundays." Through these calls, we engage in deeper conversations, with the understanding that they are a great benefit to both of us.

Before embarking on this journey, my knowledge about my maternal grandfather was extremely limited. I knew he was from Spanish Harlem, everybody called him Pete, and he dropped out of school in the second grade. I was told he had a way with words but, ironically, had never learned to read or write. Now in his eighties and coping with dementia, he brings it up every time there's an awkward moment of silence, ensuring that I know his education journey ended before the age of seven. With a playful, tender grin, he lovingly reminds me, "You know your grandfather can't read, right, baby?" And to that I reply, "Yes, Grandpa! I know."

Grandpa Pete never shares more of his story, and likely cannot now with his condition, so that's what we've all taken for fact. However, when my mother was a child, he shared with her that his motivation for abandoning his education was to earn more money to help his single mother put food on the table. Now, he imparts sentiments of sorrow and leaves it for everyone to interpret as they choose. I've always wanted to tell him that it's not too late to learn to read and write, but honestly, up until I started writing this book, I too was guilty of believing that he would never be afforded the opportunity.

While writing this book, my Soul Sunday calls with my mother grew to include more frequent conversations where I was able to ask for her assistance in gathering information about her father's childhood, something she never felt encouraged to do before. While my grandfather currently lives in a nursing home, his wife, a vibrant woman in her nineties, is still sharp enough to recall more family history than most of the people in my generation combined. I asked my mother if she could find out what part of Harlem he grew up in and where his mother was born. In a single phone call to her stepmother, she learned more than she ever had about a man she's known her entire life. The first shocker for me was the revelation that her father's name wasn't actually Pete.

"Your grandfather couldn't learn," my mother said as soon as I answered the phone one Sunday. "The school told him he wasn't capable of learning, and they sent him to a mental institution where he was institutionalized with adults." I could tell she was in complete shock, and everything she shared after that was a blur for me. At that moment, my mind raced to my circle of friends and their healthy, capable children who have been diagnosed with ADHD, ODD, dyslexia, and autism. Next, I thought about myself, who was the first in my family to be evaluated for and diagnosed with ADHD. In today's more progressive climate, although there's still a lot of room for improvement, we're able to understand the unique workings of our children's minds on a much deeper level. Yet, a shadow of sadness ultimately grew to become anger as I imagined life in the 1930s, where any child would be sent away because they lacked neurotypical learning abilities.

All these years, my grandfather simply never understood that his inability to unlock his full potential was primarily due to systemic barriers and societal limitations that existed around a lack of understanding in psychology and education, especially in Black and Brown communities. As a child, my grandfather was not illiterate because he wasn't smart. His limitations were a direct result of undiagnosed mental health challenges and a learning disability. Through my grandfather's life and his inability to share his truths, I was able to see firsthand how silence can grow to become the weapon that harms not just you but even those around you. But I can't expect my grandfather to learn or share more if no one extends an invitation to help him understand how much we now know about learning challenges.

Through my work with the Precious Dreams Foundation, I have guided tens of thousands of young people through transformative journeys, leading them to spiritual awakenings that reshape their paths, all while my grandfather aged with the belief that he was incapable of healing and learning. My disappointment in my family's silence and the realization that such simple questions had the power to uncover the truth has led me to understand even more intimately why I need to turn my attention inward and face the challenges that my family carries. They, too, deserve the same compassion and support that I readily offer to the world. My mother and her father can grow from who I've become. My family can benefit from my privileges.

Growing up, I saw my mother cry often. In the street, she embodied the quintessential Black "Nuyorican" spirit, a person of Puerto Rican origin or descent who currently or formerly resides in New York City. She often used her animated voice and Rosie Perez–like intonations to diminish any threat that came her way. If you knew my mom, you knew she was always ready for whatever and would do anything to protect herself or her family. And I mean anything. She couldn't speak a lick of Spanish, but the way she would twist her face to curse out a stranger or exaggeratedly pronounce her *r*'s showed that much of her character was built by her environment. At home, however, it was a different story. My mother was extremely soft-spoken, and her vulnerable disposition made her appear almost childlike. Her situational fragility manifested itself in different ways, allowing her to show up or shrink depending on her environment and the level of safety she felt. When she came home, it was almost as if her guard came down as she undressed. Within the confines of our home, it wasn't uncommon to see my mother express a full range of emotions, never concealing her joys or sorrows.

I was both intrigued and confused by her ability to carry herself as two different women. As a child, I studied her every move, absorbing her mannerisms like a sponge while learning how to express myself and assess safe and unsafe environments around me. Growing up, I didn't ask her many questions, not until I was sure I could support her in the sadness I believed would accompany her answers. As I reflect, there's one night that remains vivid in my memory. Looking back now with clearer and more knowledgeable eyes, it would seem as though my mother was on the brink of a mental breakdown. Without warning, she knocked on my bedroom door and announced that we would be having a sleepover. Frazzled but silent, she walked into my room with a large fold-out bed in hand, found a place right next to my bed, and positioned herself in front of my night-light to settle in. Initially, I was excited by the thought of some extra mommy-and-me time, but it quickly became apparent that something was different. Dried tears streaked her face.

"Mom, why were you crying?" I asked.

"Don't worry, baby. Mommy is okay," she responded.

"But you're not okay. What's wrong?" I didn't realize it then, but in my naive cry for answers, I empowered her to find strength of her own, the strength to acknowledge her needs. Though it wasn't my intent, it would seem as though my words were the very thing my mother needed to choose herself over everything. So, without warning, and not too many days after our emotional conversation, she packed up her belongings and left home, leaving me and my brother to live with our father without her.

This painful memory remains crystal clear in my reflections, as it left me grappling with the profound complexities of love, loss, and a broken home. It was a life-changing moment that reshaped the dynamics of our family and set me on a path toward self-comfort as I navigated my own sadness alone. On one hand, I learned the power of my inquiries, but on the other, I learned of its consequences.

Interestingly, it is around age eight that children develop the social and emotional growth to consider other people's perspectives and intentions.[3] And at age seven, I had to quickly process my mother's tears and the word "divorce," which was defined to me in some child-friendly language that I can't recall. It was as if my mother's tears were contagious, leaving me with a constant stream of my own, tears that I couldn't quite control or process. For the first few years of her absence, I'd climb into bed and cry myself to sleep, all while trying to keep as quiet as possible so neither my father nor my brother would hear me. I didn't want them to know that I was hurting. The separation of my parents marked the onset of my silence, choosing silent tears as a means of coping. I can't tell you if that technique was learned behavior, as I didn't see my father and brother openly express sorrow or suffering, but it was something I innately knew to practice.

"Silent tears," as both my mother and I often shed, refer to tears that are shed quietly and discreetly. These tears are typically a buildup of one's inner emotions and can be shed when someone is feeling sad, overwhelmed, or emotional. More importantly, they can be shed in either public or private without drawing attention to oneself. Silent tears are deeply ingrained within the complex history of Black Americans. For over four hundred years, my ancestors have chosen resilience, stoicism, and internal strength to survive. As a child, I nearly mastered this act, often crying to myself underneath the covers at night and waking up with a smile, determined to convince the world that I was okay.

For Black women, silent tears can bear a unique weight. As we navigate a world that has often dismissed or silenced our experiences, our tears stand as pillars of strength and bearers of hidden sorrows. The power of the Black woman's experience is rooted in resilience and often conceals the pain we carry. My parents were both raised by strong, single, yet stressed Black women whose sacrifices and endurance were the foundation of my family narratives. Yet, it's essential to recognize that behind their unyielding strength lies a complexity of emotions shaped by the unspoken struggles they faced.

That pivotal moment when my mom left signified the beginning of my emotional journey and an exploration of coping strategies often rooted in isolation. Since I didn't see my brother or father get emotional, I imagined they were doing the same. My brother's bedroom door was always closed, and my father was always busy fixing something or building in the backyard. When we did finally interact in our common living spaces, I could feel their sadness underneath the layer of disguise. All of us were heartbroken, but I never really knew if they were processing their emotions or simply distracting themselves to "keep it together."

About four years after my parents separated, my father's girlfriend Yolanda moved in and ultimately became my stepmom. There was something mysterious about Yolanda—not that she was secretive, but she rarely shared unless I asked. I was curious and eager to connect with her, so my questions for her were never-ending, and for some reason, whenever she told stories, I always asked, "Did they cry?" With an arched eyebrow and a hint of criticism, she would always tell me, "You love when people cry." While I'm still unpacking this in therapy, I know my love for tears had to do with my desire to see people beneath the surface. It didn't matter if the tears were on the television, from a complete stranger, or from Yolanda; there was just something about people expressing their true emotions that pulled at my heartstrings. No matter where they stemmed from, I saw tears as an invitation to further my connections and relationships with those around me. After my mother left, I found myself hungry for vulnerability, and I often ate up the slightest bit of expressed emotion like it was my last meal. I found comfort in the familiarity of tears.

In *Beloved*, one of my favorite books by Toni Morrison, she skillfully explores how both Black men and women navigate their memories, and the ways in which they're often impacted by the lingering effects of slavery. Set shortly after the Civil War, one passage illustrates the unspoken pain that my people carry even today. Morrison writes, "Saying more might push them both to a place they couldn't get back from. He would keep the rest where it belonged: in that tobacco tin buried in his chest where a red heart used to be. Its lid rusted shut."[4] Here, the characters opted to internalize their trauma to shield themselves from the things they wished not to face. Morrison's intimate exploration provided the means for me to understand how wishing the pain away with silence was a strategy that saved people—my people—from the fear of change. Generation after generation, this action in turn numbed the people around me.

Although I wished for many years that my mother had never left, as I reflect through more mature eyes, I realize that it was what was best for everyone. My love for my mother manifests itself in the way I continue to encourage her to protect her fragility. My desire is to see her heal and find an escape from the fight-or-flight energy she exuded almost daily, behaviors that likely shaped me into the person I am today. With my mom, I'm always advising; that's just the role I took on from an early age.

With this in mind, I approach each day with a balance of open-mindedness, mental stamina, and strategy. That is what it has taken for me to have tough conversations with loved ones. While every conversation hasn't led to revelations, my familial relationships have become much easier to navigate. Still, working toward initiating these conversations can be an uphill battle.

Suffering in Silence

Suffering in silence is so deeply woven into Black American culture that even today, we continue to sing about silent tears with pride. Our pain, our suffering, and our struggles are both documented and used as inspiration in our work. "Lift Every Voice and Sing," also known as "the Black National Anthem," was created in 1900 as a hymn to celebrate African American resilience and progress, and to serve as a symbol of unity and hope during a time of racial segregation and discrimination in the United States. The poem turned song became an anthem for the continued civil rights movement, and it stands as an important expression of pride, perseverance, and unity within the Black community. In this song, you can feel our reality.

God of our weary years,
God of our silent tears,
Thou who has brought us thus far on the way;
Thou who has by Thy might
Led us into the light,
Keep us forever in the path, we pray.[5]

If you look closer at your fellow humans and listen more intently to what they say, you'll notice that people all around us are suffering and experiencing increased instances of mental distress. However, suffering without words causes people to miss out on the chance for interventions and solutions for very serious issues, like abuse, domestic violence, addiction, or other adversities. Holding our suffering inside of us keeps us from healing, and that's why we all must share more.

How well can you articulate the impact of both your personal suffering and triumphs? How familiar are your loved ones with the person you've become and the art you've created (even if a mess) with your life as a result of your experiences? Despite frequent interactions, it's not uncommon to feel a sense of estrangement even in familiar company. I once went to an AYS (At Your Service) retreat in Amenia, NY with a clothing brand and 50 or more strangers. On the first night we did a reflective journaling prompt titled "If You Really Knew Me, You'd Know." We kept the responses anonymous but the host read the entries aloud so that we could recognize just how much we relate to one another. It gave everyone permission to go as deep as they wanted, and we all leaned into the responsibility of safeguarding those truths, even if it meant processing unwanted revelations about ourselves. The prompt and the experience opened up the door for us to choose to be familiar with one another not only in that space but in the days to come. I remember thinking, if I can do this in a room full of strangers, how come I can't do this at home?

In 2012, my mother and I founded the Precious Dreams Foundation. To date, we've supported over 25,000 young people with direct mental health and support services to aid in their transition both in and out of state care. It's always a challenge to convince each child that we are well-intentioned and trauma-informed certified professionals who genuinely care and want to see them succeed. We often encounter youth who, out of protective instinct, guard their pain and insecurities, fearing that revealing them will arm others with the means to exploit them further. It requires time and patience to help them understand that some people care, and we were sent, like messengers, to do the work of God.

To support ourselves, our community, and our loved ones, we must spark meaningful conversations and lean in. We must give ourselves permission to be vulnerable and reveal our truths to heal the fractures in our full body, mind, and spirit and set ourselves and our families free. We must practice telling people how we're truly doing and requesting space to share with those who give us comfort. Having little to no social support is a predominant risk factor for developed thoughts of self-harm, especially among young people.[6] No one should navigate these types of experiences alone, but we must be willing to honor our needs before we can understand how others can properly support us.

Generational Silence's Effect on Mental Well-Being

Most people navigate the world holding their words within them, often with the belief that they're taking the easier route. What they fail to realize is that unexpressed emotions and suppressed thoughts can physically manifest within our bodies and compromise our well-being over time. This is why learning emotional regulation skills and preventing emotional avoidance is so important. Remaining silent about issues that impact us and our families has pushed many individuals to the brink of mental distress, which is a leading cause of mental health disorders like depression, anxiety, post-traumatic stress disorder (PTSD), and dissociative disorders.

Think back to a time when you remained silent about an injustice or issue that directly affected you. Did you experience any of the following common signs?

- Exaggerated responses to small issues

- A lump or choking sensation in the throat

- Dissociative mental states

- Muscle tension or tightness

- Joint or body pains with no apparent known cause

- Addiction to drugs, alcohol, or other harmful behaviors

- An inability to cry[7]

The human body is remarkable and has the ability to persevere through many of life's challenges, but this resilience doesn't come without consequence. We all harbor unresolved emotions to varying degrees, but in using self-acceptance and self-compassion as our guide, we can begin to navigate both negative and positive emotions no matter how uncomfortable they make us feel, knowing that it is in our discomfort that our life forms more meaning.

Our ability to process our emotional responses to any given situation is an essential skill that we're not often taught or shown how to embrace at home. It's also worth mentioning that this skill is one that comes easier for some than others. If you're atypically brained, like my mother, it can take more effort to process emotions. Being "atypical" usually refers to individuals who are highly sensitive, creative, or neurodivergent, such as those with ADHD, Autism Spectrum Disorder, dyslexia, and other non-neurotypical conditions. According to clinical psychologist Joel Nigg, neurodivergent people can experience challenges with "emotional dysregulation," which causes them to experience greater difficulty when responding to the intensity of their emotional responses.[8] When this is the case, it might feel easier to suppress or improperly process those emotions.

Thought-stopping, the process of trying to block out negative or unwanted thoughts, and emotional suppression, the conscious or subconscious act of withholding one's feelings, are two common coping strategies that typically cause individuals to inadvertently relive traumatic experiences or suffer from the effects of suppressed emotions. Both strategies can be helpful in the short term, but eventually the negative thoughts return and can be accompanied by impaired emotional intelligence, reduced emotional awareness, and exacerbated mental disorders.[9] My grandfather is a prime example of someone who suppressed his emotions and completely blocked out the truth of a story in order to cope. As a child being forced into a mental institution with adults, I'm sure he experienced traumas that haunted him, more than likely to this day. But to cope, he suppressed these memories. In the end, it left him without the opportunity to seek and receive the support he truly needed. I'm sure many of us know someone who has experienced negative outcomes due to their perceived belief that they're better off in silence. However, the reality is their actions, or lack thereof, have the ability to cause greater harm and disconnection, possibly impacting their personal relationships and professional performance.

If you are navigating life with eyes wide open, it's easy to see the impact of slavery on communities of color. The emotional and psychological burden that Black people knowingly or unknowingly carry, although lighter than the load of our ancestors, still remains substantial today. Years of inequality and discrimination lead me to question how we got here to a silent and peaceful state, not seeking revenge but hoping for justice and hiding our pain. As I tend to the scars left by those before me, I maintain a sense of responsibility for my family and the children in my community. In the words of Maya Angelou, "The truth is, none of us can be free, until we're all free."[10] So I ask you this: What significant historical traumas or events have your ancestors experienced?

A 2023 study published in *Brain and Behavior* journal discovered that descendants of Holocaust survivors had shown stress and hormonal changes, indicating a shift in their genetic makeup, which implies that stressful events experienced by parents and grandparents can affect children even before they are born. Even after the threat has passed and the people have resettled, the body does not return to an unstressed state, and this response causes physical and psychological problems for future generations.[11] Similarly, Indigenous populations in the United States and Australia still struggle to cope with colonization, cultural erasure, and the violence committed against their communities mainly because the historical injustices and systemic inequalities aren't being fully addressed both within the community and outside of it.

Violence causes trauma, and wars against entire communities can redefine the lives of generations. Even in modern times, we often find ourselves watching helplessly as power struggles and exploitation lead to conflict around the world. Watching innocent people die, whether in our own families or communities, online, or on television, impacts us all. These memories imprint themselves indelibly in our mind and body and wreak havoc on our sense of self and safety. The only way to truly heal this is to talk. So how do you encourage family members to share their stories and talk about their emotions, especially those who have gone their whole lives without doing so?

Speaking on Trauma!

On September 11, 2001, my mother was working in her Manhattan office on Water Street when she was alerted of the first plane hitting the Twin Towers. Fearing that the US was under attack, everyone in tall buildings in the immediate vicinity moved quickly to evacuate and get outdoors. In full panic mode, my mother swiftly walked toward the towers, wanting to witness the unbelievable with her own eyes. What she saw next left her forever changed. Standing there, eyes fixated on the sky, the second plane made impact with the South Tower of the World Trade Center. As she finally turned to run, reality began to settle in: she had just witnessed a terrorist attack.

Coming from Harlem, my mother constantly witnessed violence growing up. But none of those traumatic situations compared to what she saw in the few minutes she spent evacuating her office that day. As tragedy erupted all around her, my mother, without any GPS or navigation instructions, found herself running alongside waves of people, their feet pounding the asphalt toward the Brooklyn Bridge. She recalls the bridge being so packed that it swayed from left to right, and the fear set in that she may not make it home. My mother vividly recalls the lasting emotional impact of witnessing people leap from the Twin Towers in a last effort to save themselves. September 11, the day she marks as the worst day of her life, changed the lives of many, but my mother, although privileged to be alive, was left with a version of herself that my family and I struggled to recognize.

After 9/11, my mother was diagnosed with anxiety. The fearless woman who had once navigated the world with ease now found herself gripped by panic attacks and nervous breakdowns whenever she attempted to board a plane or embark on a lengthy car ride. Growing up, there were plenty of moments when I questioned whether or not my family struggled with mental health issues, but I never had proof. My mother's diagnosis, although disappointing, was a moment that I believed would spark open conversations about mental health within our family. I was curious to learn more about my mother's brain and, by extension, maybe my own. However, to my surprise, even with a clinical diagnosis, my mother tried to hide her symptoms by keeping them to herself when she was triggered or struggling. "Outside Angie" didn't show vulnerability. Tough as nails, she couldn't afford to give anyone a front-row seat to her anxiety. And in 2001, when I didn't live with my mother anymore, it became easier for her to hide the fragile pieces of herself from me entirely.

Even if there was a desire to unpack what lay dormant deep within, my family didn't have affordable and accessible mental health solutions, and emotional development in general wasn't a priority. A roof over our heads, food on the table (most nights), and clothes on our backs were all that really mattered. When you've functioned for so long with a mentality to "just get by," shifting your perspective from survival mode to growth and development isn't so easy. It can be challenging for people to tap into their needs beyond those that are most vital.

My mother was the only other person besides myself to receive a diagnosis of a mental disorder and share it among the family, both of us receiving the news in our adult years. Between the two of us, we carry diagnoses of depression, ADHD, and anxiety. While I can say that unashamedly, I do often wonder where these conditions originated from. Although I know a traumatic event ignited my mother's anxiety, I also know that anxiety can lie dormant and remain largely unnoticed for decades until a triggering event or trauma brings it to the surface. Some individuals may have a predisposition to anxiety due to genetic or environmental factors but may not experience noticeable symptoms until they're faced with similar trauma. This is often called "latent" or "hidden" anxiety.

Seeing anxiety exhibited within my mother makes me understand the increase in undeniable symptoms that I display. When my husband is driving, I'm a high-alert and sometimes fearful passenger who is unable to trust that he can avoid every possible turn of danger. When I enter new spaces or experience new people, I often play with my hands, hoping to stay connected and distract myself from the social anxiety that's hell-bent on emerging. And more recently, I've learned that I suffer from chronic heart palpitations, which can also be a symptom of anxiety.

Speaking to my mother about anxiety, both hers and mine, used to mean waiting for her to initiate the conversation. But now that I'm intentionally tackling generational silence, I take the initiative, ensuring that I approach her with compassion and empathy. To help her disarm, I often share information that I've seen or read that may speak to the symptoms I've recognized in myself, or I may tell her about new findings she might recognize in herself. I also inquire about how she's responding to her needs and whether or not she believes her coping techniques work. This is my subtle way of offering support without actually saying, "I'm here to help," a well-meaning phrase that might trigger her to shut down.

Breaking the Mental Health Stigma in Your Family

We all know someone who can admit to needing therapy but hasn't taken the steps to make it happen. Whether they tend to get in their own way or they allow the opinions or discriminatory attitudes of others to overshadow their needs, people often find a way to make excuses or avoid getting help. Mindsets like "Therapy is too expensive," "My therapist is my best friend," "I know what I'm doing; I can deal with it myself," or even a general fear of judgment or aversion to authority are not reasons to diminish your potential and forgo professional help and thoroughly tested support services. This barrier, which some allow to be a roadblock, can decrease one's confidence and negatively impact the likelihood that they will follow through on utilizing therapeutic interventions.

Therapy is indeed expensive, but there are plenty of resources for free or discounted therapy online. I recently received free therapy through Taraji P. Henson's organization, the Boris Lawrence Henson Foundation, after searching for sponsored therapy programs and filling out a ten-minute online application. Some states like New Jersey and California offer partnerships that provide free counseling to students, and there are many nonprofits that exist solely to give communities access to mental health services. Investing time in research can help you discover programs you weren't aware of. If you want help, you can find it despite the difficulties in obtaining it.

When people approach a roadblock, there are a few ways they're likely to respond. Some simply turn around and return to their starting point, believing that the trip was not meant to be taken. Some will look for another option or route, even if it extends the trip. And then others will still try to push through before looking for alternate options as a backup. Life always gives us options, even with stigmas involved. To break any type of stigma and overcome roadblocks, you must evaluate how you're approaching each situation and whether or not you're truly determined to do what's best for you despite the difficulty.

In many communities, seeking mental health care has been perceived as a sign of weakness rather than the courageous act that it truly is. Families can fear the embarrassment or shame in admitting that there are cracks within the foundation. Particularly in Black communities, there's a deep-rooted survivalist attitude that we have everything we need. Historically, this mentality is birthed from the idea that we've endured so much and overcome without outside support, and we will be all right despite what life may bring our way. But acknowledging what's been done and seeing ourselves as capable of becoming better allows us to find strength in growing, and it gives us permission to do and be better.

You have the ability to empower your family to face their mental health support roadblocks. In everyday conversation, you can share some healing techniques (listed below) with your loved ones and ask if they are familiar with them or if they've considered trying them. These approaches, whether mentioned to explore the possibility of treatment or simply as talking points, can be valuable tools for introducing the idea of alternative approaches and promoting mental and emotional well-being in our loved ones.

- Meditation
- Regular exercise (movement) and eating healing foods daily (replacing processed ingredients with whole foods)
- Talk or sound therapy
- Support groups
- Grounding
- Art and creative workshops
- Acupuncture
- Breath work

For additional guidance on how we can approach the topic of mental health with our families, I sat down with psychiatrist and self-care coach Dr. Janet Taylor. This is what she shared:

> To break down the barriers and reduce the stigma around issues of mental health, it's critical that individuals and their families get support and education. Mental illness

is a brain-based biologic disease, not a weakness or curse, and treatable. When folks understand the why, it can lessen fear, judgment, and stigma. For someone newly diagnosed, mental illness can be confusing and generate a range of emotions. Speaking truthfully with trusted friends and family can be a wonderful resource and allow for connection and not feeling alone and isolated. NAMI, the National Alliance on Mental Illness, can provide a wealth of information for families and has local chapters for support and resources.[12]

No matter how you slice it, it all comes back to communication. Conversation is an invaluable tool to help break the mental health stigma and get ourselves and our families the help and health care we deserve. For me in particular, having these necessary conversations literally saved my life. In 2022, my mental health declined drastically due to unexpected health concerns. With sadness coming in frequent waves, threatening to drown me with every breath I took, I leaned on talk therapy to help me stay above water. I explained to my therapist that I didn't know how to cope anymore. I didn't want to journal or exercise, and I rebelled against every healthy approach I'd previously taken, feeling as if doing nothing and being completely inactive was just easier. Even though my career was built on teaching coping mechanisms to children around the world, when I was faced with difficult times, I couldn't listen to my own advice. It was a sudden and disheartening twist to go from helping others to being unable to help myself.

Throughout our sessions, my therapist gave me specific writing prompts and assignments that I had to complete between sessions, and she held me accountable to my desire to feel better. Excuses aren't accepted in therapy; instead, you are consistently tasked with looking at yourself in the metaphorical mirror for the thirty minutes or hour you meet with your therapist. While it can feel uncomfortable, I try to think of it like going to the gym. I don't necessarily enjoy the circuits, but I will be grateful for the results in the end.

One assignment from therapy that stuck with me was the request to find a childhood photo and visualize myself as that child. My therapist suggested I write out what drew me to that age, what hurt me at that age, what my child self wanted that she didn't get, and what feelings she had at the time. Doing this initially felt easy, as I picked one of my favorite photos, but as I went through the questions, I realized I had only been focusing on the moment that the image was captured and not the time frame it was taken in. I felt extremely uncomfortable examining that particular time of my life, yet processing the journey from that point to adulthood showed me that I had the power to be better for that young girl. I was no longer a powerless child, and I had to start acting like it.

Questions to Ask Yourself

Prior to engaging with others about these topics, it's important to prioritize time for self-reflection. Before taking my thoughts to others, I do my best to process them thoroughly and get clear on where I stand. Processing looks different for all of us, but I've found that introspection and self-inquiry often lead to beautiful discoveries, allowing us to form clearer judgments without being easily influenced by others' opinions. So, throughout the book, I'll pose a series of questions that are meant to spark or challenge your self-awareness. It's your choice how you answer them. You can write your responses, or they can live in the mind. Wherever you decide to place them, just make sure you allow yourself to sit with the truth. If you choose to write out your answers, I suggest also writing the question and date so you can return to your answers with a full understanding of where you were at that moment of reflection.

To what extent can I describe how my brain functions?

Just as our fingerprints are unique, so are our brains. Because no two individuals are hardwired the same, we must use our understanding of our specific anatomy to advocate for our mental needs and well-being. The brain, being your control center and the most complex organ in the body, needs love to function, and simple things, such as bodily hydration and rest, to support your mental health. The brain is made up of over 70 percent water, so if the body is even 2 percent dehydrated, it can impair your ability to perform basic tasks that require attention, psychomotor, and immediate memory skills.[13] Are you aware of the micro-decisions you make each day that positively or negatively impact your brain?

For me, knowing more about how my brain operates, especially with ADHD, has helped me figure out ways to focus better and complete tasks in which I have little interest. My understanding of myself has helped me explain to others why I sometimes get distracted and how they can better provide support for me to operate at my best. It's bridged many gaps in my personal relationships, dispelling myths and breaking stigmas. At work, my colleagues know that I prefer minimal interference and conversation so I can stay on task, and they know that if I'm not taking notes in a meeting, I will absolutely forget what next steps are required. Similarly, my friends have learned not to confuse my distracted nature with a lack of empathy or care.

My mother is continuously learning how her brain operates by examining how her anxiety functions and doing the work of uncovering techniques that help quell it. Today, she is three years free of anxiety medication. While challenges persist, the side effects were more than she could bear, so instead, she leaned heavily on establishing a holistic self-care journey. She completely changed her diet and began stretching to relieve her stress in her thirties, meditating in her late forties, and practicing yoga in her fifties. She credits all of these practices for her ability to manage her thoughts after she gained a better understanding of her needs. She also focuses on the acronym FEAR—fake evidence appearing real—which helps her understand what's really happening in her mind when fear tries to take over. The acronym reminds her to detach from the ideals that may be holding her back, those that aren't even part of reality. If my mother can overcome that in her fifties, anyone else can do the same at any time.

Do I find myself self-medicating to cope?

In the 1980s, when antidepressants hit the market, alcohol use declined.[14] This statistic reveals the truth that many people had been using alcohol to cope with symptoms of depression, but it also highlights the reality that self-medicating has the ability to make mental health issues worse. Drugs, including alcohol, provide very temporary relief, tricking people into thinking that they have control as long as they have access to the thing that gives them a "high" or relief. But in reality, their issues are taking a temporary backseat, and many times, when those negative thoughts or feelings return, they hit even harder than before, leading to yet another round of self-medication. I grew up observing how people struggle with drug and alcohol abuse, watching as my family members fell more and more dependent on the drugs each day to maintain some semblance of sanity. It's painful to watch, but it's even more painful to feel like drugs are your only option for peace of mind.

When someone decides to stop drinking alcohol, they often face questions like "What's wrong?" or "Is everything okay?" when in reality, the questioning should happen in reverse, asking those who indulge in chemical compounds that impair cognitive and motor functions if they're indeed in need of support. The harmful use of substances has multiple direct effects on adolescents and adults alike. The likelihood of unemployment, physical health problems, dysfunctional social relationships, suicidal tendencies, mental illness, and lower life expectancy is increased with substance use, even more so in adolescents. In the most serious cases, harmful use of drugs can lead to a cycle in which one's damaged socioeconomic standing and inability to develop relationships ends up feeding the substance use even further.[15]

Self-medicating to cope is an easy trap to fall into, and because of the negative stigma that's associated with it, people are often hesitant to acknowledge their truth. And since self-medicating tends to become a normal part of everyday life, it can be hard to recognize when it's happening. Here are a few signs that you or someone you know may be self-medicating to cope with life, and I've included some questions you or they can consider for each one:

- Turning to alcohol or drugs when you're feeling anxious, depressed, or overwhelmed.

    - Question to consider: Am I running from my problems today?

- Feeling the need for something stronger to feel relief over time. If it used to take one glass of wine to feel relief but now it takes three or four glasses, you may be building an unhealthy dependence and/or addiction.

    - Question to consider: Am I drinking/using drugs so it can numb my emotions or thoughts?

- Isolating from others and developing a preference to drink/use drugs alone.

    - Questions to consider: By isolating, am I trying to prevent people from seeing my struggles or dependence? If so, why?

- The idea of not having drugs or alcohol is stressful. If you find yourself avoiding social settings or situations where substances won't be available, you may be becoming reliant upon those substances.

    - Question to consider: Is this social setting a place where I can find enjoyment, even if drugs/alcohol aren't present?

- Loved ones express concerns about your substance use.

    - Question to consider: Is there some truth to their concerns?

- Your school and/or work performance is negatively impacted, and you find yourself making excuses for incomplete tasks or missing work altogether.

  - Question to consider: How could losing my scholarship or source of income impact my life and the lives of those around me?

If any of these signs of self-medication feel relatable to you and/or you're not content with your responses, I encourage you to seek professional support without delay or reach out to a loved one for help. Become okay with admitting your shortcomings so you can receive the support you need and deserve. This level of introspection is not about judging yourself harshly; rather it's about loving yourself so much that the idea of numbing your pain begins to feel like self-harm and a turnoff. Instead, opt for real, long-lasting relief, which a certified coach, therapist, or substance abuse treatment center can provide.

What barriers prevent me from speaking to my family about mental health?

Facing your mental health challenges head-on requires that you acknowledge your need for support in order to take back your life. It is not a sign of weakness to ask for help. In fact, it takes courage and bravery to step outside of your comfort zone in pursuit of a clearer heart and mind. Dr. Taylor shared with me in conversation, "If you have tried to talk about your mental health, first congratulate yourself on the effort. Resistance from family members may come from their own denial or guilt and should not stop you from engaging in conversation. You can offer to talk to them at any time, but the real focus has to be on your mental wellness. Family involvement should not be an additional stressor. Let them know how you are feeling, where you are getting care, and what medication you are taking. Modeling a positive attitude and your own self-efficacy is empowering,"[16] and that is what I call self-love.

Sometimes the tools to prepare for talks about mental health are best acquired from professionals or a loved one who possesses a deep understanding of the individual in question. Recognizing any barriers and potential facilitators for the conversation can be pivotal in paving the foundation for an open dialogue. For many, shame, guilt, or the fear of judgment or rejection can act as forceful deterrents, discouraging them from even seeking support. This is why it's essential to be empathetic and open-minded. Understand that everyone comes to these conversations with their own baggage, perspective, and awareness of self.

Strive to identify such barriers in your loved ones and tailor your interactions accordingly. One way to do this is to spark the conversation by leading with your own vulnerability. This creates a safe environment and allows the other party to feel more comfortable opening up as well. Perhaps if I had talked to my grandfather about my learning challenges and ADHD, he may have felt compelled to share his struggles in school or maybe not. I wouldn't know unless I tried. It's also important to navigate these conversations with the understanding that people will only meet you as far as they are willing to go. If the person isn't familiar with what you're sharing, they're more likely to respond from a place of ignorance. This is not necessarily a bad thing, but it could mean they need a little more education before you can engage in a meaningful conversation with them.

Healer's Recap

As we close out this chapter, I want to leave you with a few key concepts to keep in mind. In the subsequent chapters, we will build on this knowledge to get to a place where we feel confident enough to break generational silence once and for all.

- Ask your parents questions about your grandparents' mental health. If this is not an option for you, look into getting your adoption records unsealed or speak with people who knew your family personally.

- We all harbor unresolved emotions in our bodies. It's important we address them so they don't manifest in our behaviors.

- Evaluate your relationship with tears. What do you feel and what have you been taught about crying?

- Time does not heal all wounds. Sometimes the wounds that are left unhealed are passed to the next generation.

- The long-term negative impacts of thought-stopping and emotional suppression outweigh the temporary satisfaction of distracting yourself from the experience.

- Recognize when FEAR is Fake Evidence Appearing Real, then try to reframe your thoughts based on what's actually real.

- Learn, love, and invest in your brain to improve your mental well-being.

- Resistance from family members may come from their own denial or guilt and should not stop you from engaging in conversation.

Chapter Two

It's Genetic: Health Talks for Survival

Did you know that silence about generational health issues can shorten the lives of your loved ones?

Generational silence is only broken when we ask questions: questions of ourselves, of our loved ones, and of our doctors. No matter who you are, no matter what credentials you carry, the story of your life will be limited to the truths you seek out and accept. As storytellers, we are capable of owning the words to our own history. However, there are those of us who have not yet found the vocabulary to weave our honest stories together, restricted by the things waiting to be discovered around our why and the whys of the world.

Finding our truths, especially around our health, starts with releasing ourselves from our false narratives. I used to have many. Embarrassingly, I used to tell myself I could eat things that weren't good for me or talk myself out of a workout, even as I sat on the edge of my bed in gym clothes. I would reassure myself that it was acceptable to go days without seeing sunlight in order to power through fifteen-hour workdays, and I would lie through my teeth when my doctor asked how much alcohol I consumed. My professed one to two glasses a week were really closer to five or six in my twenties. Then one day I reached a point where I no longer allowed self-fibbing to create a fake reality where my lack of curiosity was harmless.

Being honest with oneself does not inherently materialize from birth. It requires a level of maturity, self-respect, and accountability to hold ourselves responsible for our BS. It involves building a relationship with ourselves that is so strong, we can be proud of ourselves, no matter what. Without a clear understanding of who we are, though, it can be just as easy to deceive ourselves as it is to deceive others. Recognizing this then helps us understand that the many things we tell ourselves often represent a singular narrative, and not an entire story, unless backed by evidence. This is why interactions and conversations with others are particularly important. If we only speak to ourselves, we'll believe anything.

Finding the truth requires deep listening, research, questioning, and data collection. The truth won't come knocking on our door or present itself in a classroom. We have to seek it by asking questions, especially when it comes to our family history and health. These questions might make some people uncomfortable, but being inquisitive shouldn't feel meddlesome or intrusive. Uncovering the truth should be the goal for everyone, especially when our health hangs in the balance.

In a very unexplainable way, life seems to slow down and escalate quickly when you're caught off guard by unexpected news. In 2022, three weeks after my husband proposed, I experienced my first lung collapse. Within a seven-month span, it collapsed three more times.

One evening, while folding clothes in my bedroom, I felt a sharp pain in my chest, followed by an immediate shortness of breath. I sat back and put my hand to my heart. It felt like something was restricting my airway, and the deeper I tried to inhale, the harder it became to breathe. I knew something was wrong, but I hoped that whatever it was would just go away on its own. For days I walked around in discomfort, hoping to avoid the financial implications and potential medical mistreatment that could incur by checking myself into the hospital. At the time, I couldn't have imagined that my lung collapsed spontaneously. As a nonsmoker and someone who sporadically engaged in exercise, I figured that, worst case, my symptoms stemmed from the COVID-19 virus.

On the fifth day of restricted breathing, suppressing the pain was no longer an option. I dropped my little sister off at school and drove myself to the nearest emergency room. At the time I didn't have health insurance. It was a monthly bill that I, and many other small business owners and entrepreneurs, tried to avoid. To dodge an exorbitant bill, I asked the doctors to skip the EKG and only check my lungs. If there's one thing Black people try to avoid, it's leaving the hospital with more problems than they came in with. Disregarding my request, the hospital followed proper protocol. They performed an EKG, followed by an X-ray of my lungs. Alone in the emergency room, I calmly waited for the results, catching up on unread text messages and revisiting old images in my photo gallery. About an hour later, the doctor ran over and blurted out, "Ms. Russell, your lung collapsed. We need to get you admitted as soon as possible." I looked at him with pure confusion and uttered a half-hearted, "Okay." If there's one thing my trauma-informed yoga certification training taught me to do well, it was to stay calm in the midst of chaos. But when he responded with an agitated, "I don't think you understand. People die from this. We have to move fast," my body flew into fight, flight, or freeze mode, as the severity of what was taking place finally registered.

The doctor's aggressive delivery about my potential death caused my body to shake so violently I could barely grip my phone. I was nervous, I was cold, I was alone, and I was quite possibly dying. While breathing remained a struggle, I slowly inhaled through my nose using the 4-7-8 technique as my one good lung fought to keep up. It was a practice that had proven effective at calming the children at my foundation, but in my current state, breathing in for four seconds, holding for seven, and breathing out for eight wasn't attainable. The voices in my head wished I didn't go to the hospital alone. The activist in me wished someone else was around to speak up, ask questions, and advocate on my behalf. I texted my husband to come fast.

My first lung collapse was treated as a spontaneous pneumothorax, a sudden collapse without any apparent cause. Without administering pain medication, doctors rushed to cut an opening through my right chest wall and forced a plastic chest tube between my ribs. To date, it's the most traumatizing thing I've ever experienced. Having a room full of physicians and students around my body, observing me like an animal in the zoo, was one thing, but them cutting into me with a knife and stabbing through the muscles between my ribs was something else entirely. It felt like intentional harm rather than necessary treatment. After many unsuccessful jabs, when the tube finally pierced my muscles, I remember instinctively grabbing for the closest nurse as if to hurt her back. Instead, I was forcefully restrained. *These people are trying to kill me*, I thought. After surgery, I was moved to a room and monitored for three days until my once-collapsed lung expanded, allowing the tube to be removed. After the excruciating procedure, I was sent home to heal with no further instructions beyond how to build back my lung capacity.

Twenty-eight days post-op, while sitting at home in a Zoom meeting, I was transported back to the painful experience of my first lung collapse. Skepticism washed over me as I calmly walked into the kitchen to find my husband Kelsei, who was in between meetings having lunch. I put my hand on my chest and said, "I think something is wrong. It's happening again." With concern written all over his face, Kelsei matched my calm demeanor and asked a couple of questions to confirm I was sure. This time, feeling a bit more aware and mentally prepared, we were able to talk through the next steps. I packed a bag and tucked away my essentials, including my journal and a book. Needing to slow down but act fast, I sat on the edge of my bed researching the top pulmonology hospitals in our state. If I was going to do this again, I needed to carefully select my provider. Still traumatized by the crummy bedside manner at the last hospital, I knew I needed a doctor who was willing to find the source of the problem. I needed a proper cause and clear diagnosis, and I could only get that by speaking up and advocating for myself.

I decided on Lenox Hill Hospital, located in a high-priced, pretentious neighborhood, to hopefully provide me with better treatment. This hospital visit was different. Not only was I in a place with more experienced care providers, but I also knew some of the staff members from a past partnership with the new health-care network and my nonprofit. While en route, I sent a text to alert them of my arrival; I needed them to be prepared. Once admitted, I was put on a VIP list and given the best care I'd ever received at any hospital in my entire life. I felt safe, but at the same time, I felt guilt. Even with the comfort of knowing my care might be prioritized, I couldn't help but think about those who lacked economic privilege or personal connections. I shared their trauma, and it felt unfair being on the other side.

Being a woman often proves to be a disadvantage in emergency rooms across the US. Studies show that women wait twelve minutes longer, on average, to be evaluated and treated in an emergency room than men, sometimes to devastating consequences.[1] And another study published in *Women's Health* (London) journal in 2022 showed that Black women waited 46 percent longer than white women in emergency rooms for pregnancy-related problems.[2] This is just one reason why I traveled outside of my community for elevated care. It's been embedded in me that all care isn't equal. Black Americans, women, and other marginalized groups have persistently experienced unequal treatment when seeking medical care. This reality has led to centuries of negative health outcomes and an increase in preventable deaths.

The next day at Lenox Hill, after I arrived for my emergency pleurectomy to reattach my lung to the chest wall, the doctors performed a biopsy. While in recovery, a new doctor visited me and asked if I had any instances of endometriosis in my family. To my shock, I had no idea. She then began to explain the symptoms, which included painful menstrual cramps, back or shoulder pain, pain during intercourse, infertility, and in extremely rare cases, lung collapses. Immediately, I thought of my grandma Geri, who had four miscarriages before she had my mom and suffered from debilitating cramps. While her symptoms were often dismissed as nothing more than a difficult period, was it possible that what she struggled with was undiagnosed, untreated endometriosis? And since it is more likely for those with family members who have endometriosis to also be diagnosed with it, was it then possible that I had dealt with this my entire life too?

My pain had been overlooked for ages. I still remember the feeling of lying on cold bathroom tiles as a teenager, curled up for comfort during every menstrual cycle. In pain, I'd lie there and moan as time passed by, hoping to make it back to bed once my pain relievers kicked in. Each period came with excruciating pain, and on a handful of occasions, I ended up being admitted into the hospital. With each visit, I was simply given a high dosage of painkillers to pacify the issue and was sent home. Not once did a doctor even present endometriosis as a possibility. I grew up believing I was just one of many teenagers who had terrible cramps, heavy periods, and limited options. Learning about endometriosis two decades later was a bittersweet experience. I felt like I had been gaslit, intentionally or not, by both loved ones and medical professionals my entire life. However, I was also grateful to finally be able to name the pain I had been suffering from for so long. My grandmother didn't have this privilege.

Currently, the only way to give someone an accurate endometriosis diagnosis is to see a lesion through laparoscopic surgery. That means a clear diagnosis requires surgery. This is partly why six out of every ten cases of endometriosis go undiagnosed and why I felt the need to share my story here. Hopefully this information will empower you to talk to your loved ones about their menstrual cycles or turn to your doctors to learn more. If the medical establishment does not have women's best interests in mind, then it's up to us to do the leg work of keeping ourselves well and properly informed.

Through this traumatizing experience, I suffered so much confusion, but I didn't even know what questions to ask because every part of the process felt so unfamiliar. Thankfully, the doctors at Lenox Hill began to ask *me* questions, and I began to learn that what I considered to be unfortunate circumstances were actually endometriosis symptoms. All it took was about two minutes for me to piece together decades of confusion. I received an official thoracic endometriosis diagnosis, and I slowly connected the health stories and histories of my family to my current state. With a clear understanding of my experience, I now feel equipped to say, I have endometriosis, and I do not believe I am the first woman in my family to have it. We are having a human experience with the cells of our ancestors, so it's imperative that we learn their history to better understand who they are and what they were up against, especially as Black and Brown people.

Strategies for Developing a Better Relationship with Your Health Practitioner

Contrary to what you may have been told, you do not have to settle for mediocre health care, and you have the power to set the tone for a productive conversation at the doctor's office. Conversations with your physician might feel rushed or unwelcome, but remember that you and/ or your health insurance are covering the cost of the visit, so you should get what you need out of it. You deserve premium care.

Don't be afraid to speak up, advocate for yourself, and ask questions when it comes to your body and health. When we lean into silence, we strip ourselves of these rights. Speaking up empowers us to take back control of these conversations, and it forces doctors to truly slow down and see us as human beings seeking real answers. One of the biggest lessons I learned through my many doctor visits is to ask questions that allow physicians the opportunity to explain what they know. To accomplish this, however, we must be delicate with our approach. Make sure that the pain, discomfort, or challenges that brought you to the doctor's office are properly expressed but aren't overshadowed by impatience or irritability, which can be reflected in our tone. These behaviors often spark a negative response.

Before my post-surgical follow-up appointments, I would write out my questions in advance to prevent them from feeling like an interrogation. Even though I had been contemplating them for weeks, I wanted my conversation with the doctor to feel like one truth seeker communicating with another truth seeker so I could live. Here are some of my communication strategies for productive health-care visits:

Avoid "YOU" statements.

When speaking with any person managing your care or the care of a loved one, try to start sentences with "I" rather than "you." "You" statements are often translated as accusatory comments and don't often lead to the best outcomes. Dr. Thomas Gordon, an award-winning psychologist widely known for teaching communication skills, categorized what he calls "I" messages in the following ways: (1) a brief, non-blameful description of the behavior you find unacceptable, (2) your feelings on the matter, and (3) the tangible and concrete effect of the behavior on you.[3]

An example of this in the health space would be something like: "I feel frustrated. I waited an hour to be seen, and this has thrown off my schedule." This lets the doctor know how you're feeling without pointing the finger. The opposite of this would be something like: "You made me wait an hour to see you." This comes off as accusatory and unfair and blames the doctor for the inconvenience.

Be vulnerable but calm.

It's important that you ground your emotions on even the most serious matters to the best of your ability. This will allow you to avoid raising your voice, becoming offensive, or making unnecessary accusations. If you're unable to ground your emotions, be honest about them. For example, tell your doctor, "I'm afraid. This really worries me," and then transition into your questions. Try to focus on gathering pertinent information, and check the unnecessary comments or emotions at the door.

Instead of asking abrasive questions like "Why should I trust you?" or "Shouldn't you know how to fix this?" you can ask, "How confident are you that this remedy will garner positive results for me?" or, "Have any of your patients reported negative or unusual symptoms from this medication?"

Treat your doctors like people, and they will do the same.

In 2022, my conversations with doctors lasted longer than all of the previous years combined. As I openly asked more questions and received helpful answers, medical professionals became people I learned to trust and care about. After all, these people are partially in charge of my well-being. For my sake and theirs, it was only right that I let down my guard and walk into their spaces with an open heart and mind. Simple mindset shifts to raise their vibrations, like asking how they were doing, making small talk, and giving positive energy, have made such a difference in my outcomes. After all, your doctor is in the practice of opening doors all day, and they never know who's on the other side. Why not initiate kindness in case they fail to or need a reminder?

Taking the time to build a rapport with your doctor not only makes asking health questions a bit easier, it also reminds them that you're not just a block on their calendar. With each exchange, it shows them that you're a patient anticipating their care. Through the simple act of speaking up and sharing truths, you set yourself up for success.

In speaking candidly with Dr. Chu, my endometriosis specialist, I learned that women and young girls with endometriosis have a significantly higher chance of developing heart issues than women without it. These women are 62 percent more likely to have a heart attack, develop chest pain, or require heart procedures to open blocked arteries.[4] Knowing this helped me prioritize seeking out a cardiologist when I noticed arrhythmias (an irregular heartbeat), which was something I had never dealt with prior to my first lung collapse.

You know the saying "If it's not one thing, it's another"? Well, that began to define most of my days after my heart started acting up. I was instructed by my doctor to wear a heart monitor, which showed that I had an extra heartbeat 7 percent of the time. Many arrhythmias are harmless, but mine was a concern for my cardiologist. To gain a better understanding of my condition, doctors at Lenox Hill asked me if I had a known history of heart disease or heart-related issues in my family. At the very least, I knew that my mother and my grandma Geraldine both had heart surgery. I also believe I was told at some point that my grandpa Pete had heart issues as well. Not knowing much more about their health outside of that, I felt a sense of shame for my ignorance. Suddenly, I found myself questioning everything about myself and my soon-to-be healing journey. How well do I understand everything I've inherited from the people who made me? How much trauma am I carrying from past and present racial disparities that exist within the United States health-care system?

I ended 2022 with four major emergency surgeries, eleven new scars, a couple medical malpractices, a handful of unexpected diagnoses, and a vast awakening. Health talks save lives, and I encourage everyone to start having them before it's too late.

Being Proactive and Asking Preventative Questions

Have you ever regretted a missed opportunity to ask questions? When we lose a loved one, we mourn so much more than their physical body. Every death robs us of wisdom, untold stories, and knowledge about our familial health—voids left behind by their absence. I like to compare the lost history as having the answer to a long math equation but not being able to see the work that was done to get to the solution.

Since navigating my health journey, I've become more curious about the passing of my ancestors and have begun seeking justice for them and future generations by fighting to live with the proper tools, along with physician accountability. I wonder just how many people in my family would have lived longer or healthier lives if they had adequate care or the resources to learn about their symptoms. Knowing our health options and autonomy is just as important as knowing our rights.

Eager to dive back into the deep end of my ancestral pool of knowledge, I found myself being magnetized by my main source of knowledge, my mother, as she was the person who knew Grandma Geraldine the best. To fill in her health gaps, I reached out to my mom via text: "Hi, Mom, do you have ten minutes? I would love to talk with you about our health history." Texting to get permission helped me ease into what might've been a tough or triggering talk for her. Since my grandmother's passing, my mom has struggled to cope, and the last thing I wanted was to keep bringing her to a place of sadness with my inquiries. My mother accepted my invite to a conversation, only for me to realize that I wasn't prepared. Instead of a freeform conversation, I realized I needed to organize my thoughts with questions: "How much can you tell me about our family health history?" and "Did you have health talks with your parents when you were a child, and if so, what did they teach you?"

I really wanted to start with "What can you tell me about grandma's health issues?" but that would've been too abrasive. I've found that starting with more general questions leads to responses that signal whether a person is willing to open up and go deep. I called and, without hesitation, asked my mother how much of our family's health history she could confidently explain. With sadness and disappointment in her response, she admitted she had limited knowledge of her family's health history. "I know that my mother's mother, my grandmother, died of an aneurysm. She was in her fifties. From what I understand, my grandfather died of natural causes in his late seventies. My mom came home from work and found him in a chair. On my dad's side, my grandmother died in her sleep of natural causes, too."

She paused, either because she felt that was enough sharing or she was reaching for more information. During the silent moment, I asked if there was ever an autopsy performed for my great-grandmother who died of natural causes. My mother wasn't sure. She continued to share but transitioned into what she knew well—her mother's history. She explained that Grandma Geri, whom I called Grandma G, had a lot of health issues that included problems with her heart. She had everything from high blood pressure to colitis. She also had a tilted uterus, which is why, my mom explained, she couldn't bear children. After four miscarriages, she was finally able to have my mom. She had ulcers, diabetes, multiple surgeries, and was only fifty-one when she had her first heart attack. Not one known to eat well, she also didn't have the education to understand how her eating habits could negatively impact her health.

As my mother continued, I grabbed my journal to take notes. I kept them short so I wouldn't get too distracted or miss anything important. I made sure to write down the words "tilted uterus" and "heart attack" because I knew I wanted to circle back to those phrases once my mom was finished speaking. I had learned from personal research that a tilted uterus does not impact a woman's ability to conceive. And if this is what my grandmother was told, it would make sense why she didn't continue advocating for a proper diagnosis. When my mother finished speaking, I shared the myth about the tilted uterus, and her reply was nonchalant: "Oh, well, that's what they told her." Because that was such a pervasive understanding, not only in their community but also from the medical professionals they interacted with, it is no surprise that that explanation was what my mother carried as the reason for my grandmother's infertility issues. Over time, it became what they held as unfailingly true.

One thing I know about truths is that sometimes it's difficult for people to accept them, especially if what they believe to be true came from people they love and trust, or someone who is no longer here. So while I always do what I can to share my truths, I never try to force them on anyone else. I was content with knowing that my mother could form her own opinion based on my learnings and the thoughts of my grandmother's physician from the 1960s.

I moved on to my second question, asking my mother how much her parents talked to her about health and how that information, or lack thereof, impacted her life. My mother shared that neither parent had talked to her about health. She ate whatever she wanted, and everything she wanted to learn, she had to teach herself. It wasn't until she was fifty-two, when she found herself going down the same road as her mother, that she fully adopted a healthier lifestyle. With some of her challenges, including obesity, high blood pressure, and sleep apnea, it was evident that change was needed. With no advice or example to follow, she educated herself on the body and discovered why eating healthy was so important. I witnessed this shift in her as a young adult, but I wasn't aware of the discipline and strength it took for my mother to break the cycles passed down by her parents, which existed long before she found herself at a similar crossroad.

In conversations with my mother, I learned that her true motivation for changing her lifestyle was not only to live but to live well. She didn't want to become dependent on medication (at least not all of them). "Your grandmother was on eleven medications every single day to maintain stable health. I used to be on six. Today, I'm not on any. Food healed me, and slowly I stopped needing a lot of my medications." As we talked, my mother's emotions suddenly shifted, focusing on her personal health journey. In turn, she also grew more comfortable sharing her learnings. She was proud of the work she put in to have a better life.

I thanked my mother for being an example that our genes don't have to determine our fate. I expressed gratitude for what she's been able to do for herself and for everything she's shown me. I ended the conversation letting her know that I not only appreciated the talk but that her knowledge was useful for me, and I hoped it would inspire her to speak more candidly in the future. We quickly shifted the conversation to the more general health issues around systemic discrimination and began exchanging experiences. It was a quick vent about the ways of the world we'd love to improve. Racial bias and systemic issues are not topics we often cover in our regular check-ins, but the health talk made it easier to go there. I appreciated that our initial conversation about family health led to us sharing our thoughts about important topics we didn't usually discuss.

My first intentional health talk was a success. When the call ended, I sat for a bit with my mother's responses. Alone with my thoughts, I could fully digest her words, and I started thinking about the meaning of "natural causes." Natural causes are deaths that weren't caused by external factors. It can mean nearly any medical condition or form of cancer. Why wouldn't we push for more answers to prevent such "causes" from showing up in future generations? I wondered how many "natural deaths" could've been put off a bit longer. Our health talk gave me even more motivation to fight for my family's wellness.

When you begin doing research and having these talks with family members, you won't remember to ask everything in the first conversation. More questions will come with time, but be gentle with your curiosity. It's important to remember that not everyone is on the same journey as you. Although your intentions are selfless, the conversations you have may inspire others to have their own revelations, and you should give them grace and time to sit with their thoughts. After speaking with my mother, I needed time for reflection, and I believe she did too. When I called the following day, I only checked in to ask how she was doing. I left the floor open for her to revisit the health topic if she wanted, but she didn't, at least not for a while.

Questions for Your Family and Loved Ones

Talking to your loved ones about their health history can force them to remember moments, places, and people that spark all types of emotions. It can also teach them how much they don't know. There's no predictable outcome, but it's always worth the risk. To manage these types of difficult conversations, you must remember the four Ps: be **P**atient, never **P**ushy, and always **P**ractice **P**eace. Who in your family might be open to a health talk? You don't have to start with a parent or grandparent; it could be anyone who is familiar with family history. Like my conversation, start with two general questions and zero expectations.

Here are some examples of questions that could lead to a productive conversation. I encourage you to choose the two that speak to you the most, and use those as a jumping-off point for the conversation to come.

- How much can you tell me about our family health history?

- Did you have health talks with your parents, and if so, what did they teach you?

- Do you know if there are any diseases or medical conditions that run in the family?

- Do you deal with any invisible illnesses? Do you have any fears when it comes to your long-term health?

- Do you know if I had any physical health challenges as a baby?

- What has been the biggest health concern in our family?

If you're speaking in person or over video chat, ask if you can take notes, so the person understands why you're not giving them your undivided attention. Taking notes or recording audio will help you retain the information or think of future questions. To be a good listener, focus on writing key words, not complete sentences.

On this journey, I've had discussions with all types of people. Most were willing to talk, but not everyone, for any number of reasons. One thing I learned is that no two people need the same type of approach. So, what happens if the person you want to speak with doesn't want to speak with you? In discovering additional ways to meet people with compassion, I tapped Anna Tubbs, my friend and *New York Times* bestselling author of *The Three Mothers: How the Mothers of Martin Luther King, Jr., Malcolm X, and James Baldwin Shaped a Nation*. She provided the following advice: "The best place to start is to try to figure out what is keeping the person from sharing. Is it that they experienced something traumatic that they don't want to relive? When you have a better understanding of where they might be coming from, you can start to frame your questions differently so you are careful to either leave some questions out, or you can word questions to affirm the value of the person's answer and showcase your genuine interest."[5] To Anna, most people will feel at ease with an easy and approachable opening.

Believe it or not, people like talking about themselves. According to *Scientific American*, "On average, people spend 60 percent of conversations talking about themselves, a figure that jumps to 80 percent when communicating via social media platforms.[6] Sharing personal reflections or information produces the highest level of activation in neural regions associated with motivation and gratification, so never fear asking someone to speak about themselves.

A good way to do this is by starting with icebreaker questions like "Is there a place in the world that you really want to go to but haven't been?" "What was your favorite class or subject in school?" or "Did you ever break a bone or have a serious physical injury as a child?" If these questions don't work, respect their boundaries and accept that they are not ready to share right now.

For many Black Americans, information about our family's history is often distorted, severely limited, or missing altogether for a variety of reasons. If you don't have access to family members or biological parents, there are alternative ways you can learn your health history:

- Talk to someone who knew your family and ask what they can recall.

- Ask your doctor about clinical genetic testing so you can learn whether you have hereditary diseases hidden in your DNA. You can also contact a genetic counselor who can answer any questions you may have about the results.

- Use your birth parents' names and birthdays to find public records, such as birth or death certificates. These documents can be requested online through your local Department of Health or Office of Vital Records. For *The Three Mothers*, with the help of local historians, Anna was able to gain access to both birth and death certificates for the research needed to put multiple family stories together.

As you collect information, always remember that stories are not facts or full pictures. Your new insights will require further research, and the internet is another great resource. When I first found out about my diagnosis, I knew there wasn't a family member who could guide me on how to turn things around or improve my situation. My mother didn't have endometriosis, and she never struggled with the symptoms. So I turned to online groups and social media pages led by medical professionals or people with similar experiences for support. Through my initial hashtag search, I discovered Endo Black on Instagram, a Black advocacy page for women with endometriosis. Not only did I feel more informed, but the founder, Lauren Kornegay, was open to meeting with me via Zoom to share even more information. I also gained community, using Direct Messages to connect with other endometriosis warriors.

After connecting with over a dozen complete strangers on social media, it was suggested that I continue the support talk by joining a Facebook group called Thoracic Endometriosis/Lung Group. Both groups have helped me feel less alone, and although none of these women can advise me on what's best for my body, I can learn from their stories and, in turn, use those examples to guide my own decisions.

Find your tribe. Social media houses support groups for nearly everything. Try doing a search on Facebook groups with some of the keywords you noted from conversations with family members. You may need to filter through or join multiple groups until you find the best fit, but the one thing you'll discover is that you're not alone. You'd be surprised how comforting it can be to talk to a stranger or a community of people who know your pain.

Lastly, keep track of your findings. Your ancestors and loved ones who are no longer with us can live through the stories you tell today. And finding the root cause and path to one's death is imperative to the future success of any family. Sharing real, true stories will save people, primarily when they're centered around the reasons we die. We're not just here to survive; we're here to live. And life shouldn't be cut short because of repeated cycles of pain and discomfort. My mother is alive because she chose a lifestyle that would guarantee better circumstances.

As I approach life through a new lens, I feel like I've started to become a better friend to my mother. I recognize that we're both committed to breaking unhealthy patterns within our family. Using the tools we've inherited, my mother and I are grasping the concepts of self-advocacy and putting our learning into practice. We're challenging health-care providers and seeking second opinions, which is something our ancestors didn't always have the privilege to do. It's one of many steps needed on this journey of total healing, and the impact will be greatest for future generations. Breaking generational cycles isn't for personal fulfillment; it's for the family. What if we all made conscious decisions to communicate about generational health issues *before* people got sick? What a revolutionary act that would be!

If there's one thing I've learned, it's that people should ask questions before challenges arise, and the most appropriate time to ask questions is today, when a person is alive, of sound mind, and willing to talk. Please don't wait until they're sick, under the influence, or forgetful. Don't wait until there's an emergency like I did. And even if you do and you're guilty of waiting to heal like me, it doesn't mean it's too late.

Questions for Yourself

As you gather new information from your doctors and loved ones, it's imperative to also look within. When people experience consistent pain over long periods of time, they tend to grow a higher tolerance for it. When you're a part of a race of people that has been systematically under-treated for pain (physically or mentally), it's common to start downplaying it yourself. I've had painful periods and ovarian cysts for over a decade, yet I had been overlooked by my doctors during each of my yearly check-ups. When a particularly gruesome cyst erupted when I was twenty-three, not only was I ill-prepared, but I also didn't ask questions, so the medical professionals treated me as if it was a one-off, random freak occurrence. But what if I disrupted the pattern of generational silence by simply following up or proactively seeking a second opinion? The answers to those questions, as well as my awareness of and trust in my body, could have helped me navigate—or avoid—the traumatic diagnosis I later received.

Become better acquainted with yourself. The best decision I made in 2022 was to start a health journal. It's a great way to check in with yourself and become more conscious of what your body is experiencing. You don't have to write in it every single day but try to at least once a week. In your health journal, ask yourself the following questions:

- How does my body feel today?

- What have I done to contribute to these feelings?

- Is my body trying to tell me something? If so, what?

Another purpose of a health journal is to keep your personal medical history, as well as that of your family members, in one place. Your journal can then be passed down to future generations so they, too, can take control of their health. Here is how I formatted my health history pages:

Date:

Description of Physical or Mental Symptoms:

Health Discoveries:

Health Questions:

Professional Diagnosis or Medical Results:

Thoughts:

This journal is only the beginning. It's a promise for future generations that you will leave them well and better than where you began. It's a way of telling your family and those who come after you that you love them, too.

Healer's Recap

- Understanding our family members' bodies can help us nurture and care for our own.

- Start somewhere. Death certificates are public records, and in some cases, they're easy to find online.

- Hold on to obituaries.

- Ask your doctor questions, even if you feel rushed. It's better to ask when you have the chance than to wait until your next appointment.

- We are having a human experience with the cells of our ancestors. Feel empowered to learn what you're carrying.

- Talk to your relatives. Ask delicate questions and take notes (if allowed).

- Knowing your family health history can lead to early detection by guiding doctors to test for medical problems when you present warning signs.

- If you're adopted or can't find the answers you're looking for, use this frustration to start writing your story. Your health, history, and words can break cycles for future generations.

- Keep a health journal of medical records and genetic disorders. Keep it safe and know that one day it will be read by someone who needs it.

Chapter Three

Just Getting By

Did financial obligations impact the way your parents showed up during your childhood?

During a rocky period in my parents' marriage, they moved my brother and me from a co-op building on Metropolitan Avenue in the Bronx to a three-bedroom family home with a front and backyard in Long Island. I was happy in the Bronx, where the vibrant culture and busy streets were all I knew, but I didn't realize how good more space would feel. While there were many differences between the two living situations, the biggest win of all was that I would no longer have to share a bunk bed with my brother. In our new home, I had my own space for the first time, and my mind was now open to new circumstances. As a child, I thought homeownership set my family apart from poverty. Through my young eyes, our home was a symbol of hard-won stability amidst economic challenges.

Moving to the burbs and owning a house meant my mother would no longer have to drive around for two hours each night looking for parking. We now had the luxury of a driveway, and on the cold, snowy days, we could even park the car in our garage. If you know anything about NYC street parking, you know how much a driver's life revolves around searching for a spot and adhering to early morning alternate-side parking regulations, all while wasting hours and gas in this convoluted pursuit. I'll never forget the one night a man threatened my mother after stealing the spot she desperately waited on for a half hour. She responded to that threat by exiting the car wielding a club, signaling for my brother to run upstairs and get my father. Luckily that altercation didn't escalate too much further beyond the initial exchange, but I thought the man was really going to fight my mother over the spot. In the Bronx, it was typical for neighbors to argue over parking spaces, and it was seemingly common for men to intimidate women with children, further emphasizing my parents' desire for a new environment.

In my eyes, moving to Long Island meant we were thriving, even if, in doing so, money got tighter and the monthly mortgage payments prevented us from eating out or buying toys beyond Christmas. I knew my father's aunt, my great-aunt Genny, was helping us make the move happen, but I didn't know why or how much she had invested. Still, it was clear that growing from a modest-sized two-bedroom apartment with bunk beds to a three-bedroom home with a separate dining room and basement that needed furnishing would be quite a financial challenge.

Though money is often a necessity, and even life-changing, as a child, what I craved most was time and attention, and it was easy to feel the love when both of my parents lived in the house. When my father worked nights, my mother was home, and when my mom was at work during the day, my father was home. We even sat down together at the dining room table for meals. It was everything I had seen growing up on TV. At just six years old, I'd already grasped that the presence of family and quality time was what truly made a house feel like a home. However, when my parents split a little over a year after we moved into our new house, my mother's sudden absence meant that both of my parents were now required to make many sacrifices in order to fulfill their financial obligations without a joint income.

During the early stages of their separation, and prior to legally filing for divorce, my father went into an unimaginable amount of debt. His financial decisions initiated a ripple effect that extended all the way to my mother. Under the law, she was still legally his wife. Consequently, with the stain of debt impacting her credit, she faced considerable challenges when trying to rent an apartment and rebuild her life after divorce. Even as a child, I could feel the everlasting impact this ordeal had on her mental health, but looking back it might've felt more intense to my child self because she would often vocally complain about the situation.

The financial stress forced my mother back into survival mode, a place she hadn't been in a while. This made her feel resentful, and during my weekend visits with her, she often voiced her disappointments and anger. Her frustration was obvious; she simply couldn't conceal it. She talked about how my father's decisions adversely affected her and followed it up each time with "but you don't even know the half" or "but that's not for you to know." My mom struggled to maintain her composure and felt like her world was out of her control. On the flip side, my father reserved his feelings for others, never venting to my brother and me and only showing an occasional eye roll if I shared news about my mother's new life. His actions said a lot on their own, but I appreciated his composure. I didn't want to hear anything negative about either one of them; they both meant so much to me.

As money got tighter around our house, I became more resourceful. Winter coats got recycled year after year, and I mixed and matched my school clothes so creatively that it looked like I had different options each week. Despite my initial misjudgments about the state of my family's finances, at age seven, I could feel that I had less than my peers in school. Aside from my feelings of lack within a community of middle-class families, I was frequently teased for wearing "skippies," a frugal sneaker choice, and "no name brand" clothing. Yet, I wasn't ashamed. Regardless of what anyone thought of my possessions, I knew I was going home each day to a clean home, and that my parents were doing the best they could.

We learned very quickly how to stretch each dollar, and we especially learned how to make leftovers last. I remember far too many days where boredom and a growling stomach would lead me to the refrigerator. In front of minimal options, often thinking I would find something new with each visit, I would just stand there and pout.

On those days, I experienced a sense of resentment, reflecting fondly on the times when I had both parents in the home, and we had complete and balanced meals. Although my brother and I appreciated every penny earned through my father's tireless labor, I often found myself wishing for my mother's return.

Traditionally, being the head and only parent of a household meant you had to sacrifice quality time and patience in order to invest time into generating revenue. Though my father was the embodiment of hard work, at home his presence was subdued and anxious, with his mind constantly tallying the next expense or how long my brother and I were keeping on the lights in each room. As a child, I wished I could help, but I knew I couldn't. I was simply too young. To me, money appeared to be the magical cure for life's problems since its absence brought only stress and friction among people who couldn't do enough for each other.

My parents didn't come from money, nor did they know too much about how to manage it. On both branches of my family tree, resilience, not financial aptitude, was a common thread. On my father's side, my grandmother managed to raise four children on her own on a limited budget obtained through cleaning houses, and on my mother's side, my single grandmother, who lost her parents at a young age, faced the world alone, learning to overcome life's hurdles in a constant state of survival. Both women raised families on one income.

You couldn't necessarily see our financial strain from the outside looking in, but once inside you could tell that times were hard. With our boiler always broken, our main heat source was an open stove from the day we moved in until the day I went off to college. At night, we slept with our bedroom doors open as the heat from the stove rose and filled our home. Despite these hardships, a part of me lived in a perpetual fantasy that we were a middle-class family because we were homeowners, a dream for many Americans.

Education Matters

My parents prioritized having a consistent, reliable income regardless of what the job entailed. They didn't know much about money, but they knew about the consequences of not having enough. In their youth, financial health was not a conversation at home or a standard part of the educational curriculum in school, a gap felt more acutely in Black communities. The absence of Black educators and targeted financial education for Black children meant that my parents, like many others, entered adulthood unprepared, without substantial knowledge of how to manage their money.

People teach what they know, which I believe was the motivation behind my great-aunt Genny helping my father with his homeownership journey. Her philosophy was all about achieving and then reaching back to pull up the rest of the family. In contrast, there weren't any homeowners in my mother's family for her to turn to. Without many resources for healthy money habits, like many other Black people at the time, my parents found themselves working hard for less and always praying for more.

My stepmother, Yolanda, would often stop at the corner store on her way home from work to try her luck with the lottery. Although she prayed for sheer luck, and even hoped to dream up some lucky numbers, nobody fell into a large sum of money by chance. When Yolanda moved into our basement a few years after my mom left, I remember my father using Christmas as a reason to splurge on scratch-offs. I'd never seen him do this with my mom, so I figured it was something Yolanda enjoyed. With each ticket, they hoped against the odds for a win that would uplift the entire family. Curled up beside her, I watched as she scratched ticket after ticket with a mix of hope and anxiety. With the luck of a good scratch, we could become millionaires.

When Yolanda moved in, things improved a bit. She didn't cook for the family, but on Fridays she would buy us Pizza Hut, which happened to be our favorite local cuisine. We looked forward to that pizza all week long, and on the weeks when she forgot, I made sure to give her a reminder. My brother would come into my room and say, "Are you going to ask her?" to try and encourage me to go down to the basement and try our luck. She almost always said yes, but still for some reason, he was nervous to ask.

Poverty and financial hardship are layered phenomena, and finding solutions necessitates education and a hustle mentality. We're fortunate when knowledge is voluntarily passed down from one generation to the next, but it's impossible to pass down what you don't know. This is why embracing a philomath mindset is essential. A "philomath" is someone who craves and desires constant learning. Adopting this mindset is necessary in order to acquire the knowledge we seek; it will empower you to, among other things, ask unsolicited questions of your family members and people around you. And it may even spark their own curiosity for the unknown.

Do you know if your parents' actions, opinions, and mindsets surrounding money were learned from childhood or reactions and perspectives rooted in fear? Before writing this book, I had limited knowledge about how my parents were raised, but I did know that my father grew up in a home that was purchased by his parents. As a result, he fought to give my brother and me the same opportunity he had. What I didn't know was that our family home was the first house my mother had ever lived in. I never knew or thought to ask about her assets as a child, as my limited perspective was focused on what they were doing for me (typical kid!).

Great parents will work to give their children a better life. With my mother being a cofounder of Precious Dreams Foundation, I always understood that her inspiration for wanting to start the foundation was my little sister Miracle. She never mentioned a more personal connection to the work. Yet, sometime around the tenth anniversary of our work, when I was about thirty-five years old, I learned she, too, was homeless as a teenager. Despite my daily work as the foundation's executive director and the reflections that I would share about my days addressing homelessness and poverty, these topics never prompted her to reveal her personal journey. My grandmother instilled in her that this chapter of her life was a private one, so private that she went on to hide it from everyone throughout her adulthood, even me.

During this time of my mother's life, my grandpa Pete was around, but he didn't live in the same house or contribute financially to the household. When my grandmother Geri faced job insecurity, she and my mother were forced to couch surf with friends and family until they could get back on their feet. At the time, she felt a sense of shame, but in the comfort that developed from our Soul Sunday conversations, one day she just decided to open up. I didn't ask any questions to prompt this story, but I think the more we began to talk about her childhood, the more my mother felt safe to share, and perhaps the more these stories released themselves from the recesses of her heart and mind.

"I never shared this with anyone, not even your father," my mom shared. "I just didn't feel comfortable telling people, and your grandmother was very stern and adamant that what happened in the house stayed in the house. We kept family secrets to ourselves. There's a lot I still haven't told anyone." I wish I could pull out the many years of shame and secrecy that my mother has held in her body, not just from her own experiences but from the generations before her. I wish to teach them that the stigma only grows in silence, and that their truth could've been a teaching moment for many. I wish they knew that homelessness doesn't have a face, and that it was a tremendous accomplishment for my mother to break that cycle of housing insecurity for her children.

The trauma that comes with burying truths can often cause more harm than good. Learning from my mother's actions and acknowledging what worked and didn't shaped the way I show up for myself. Although I was afraid to tell people about my struggles when I was in the midst of them, I managed to find the courage, even in my weakest moments, because deep down I wanted help, and I knew it could make a difference. I knew that help sometimes changes lives.

In 2022, I sat on a Zoom call with Bernadette, one of the Precious Dream Foundation's board members. I was still in recovery mode from my surgeries and feeling anxious about potentially more bad luck or unlucky health news lurking around the corner. I started the meeting that day aiming to keep it together and get right to business. I was not prepared for her to genuinely ask me how I was doing. I tried to answer with a short response and move on, but she wanted to dig deeper. She began to acknowledge my challenges and asked how I was coping. Within two minutes, I fell apart, crying in front of the woman I do business with. While I never imagined the help I was craving could come from an associate, I was grateful that she pried. Bernadette suggested that I visit a holistic doctor, someone who previously helped her family. As I declined, expressing that I couldn't afford the out-of-network visit, she offered to cover the cost of a consultation. Imagine if I hadn't allowed myself to release and share in that moment. Bernadette wouldn't have had the opportunity to offer such a generous gift, and I wouldn't have met the man who I believe helped me heal and embrace my fertility journey.

Desperate for a more natural approach to my recovery, I was geeked to speak with someone who would take my mind, body, and spirit into consideration. I was craving a whole-body approach because nothing I was doing seemed to heal the isolated areas within me that experienced the most trauma. During my first visit, Michael Pizhadze studied the wave frequency of my organs on a cellular level through what he calls a Matrix Decoder. He was able to find imbalances all over my body and called them out one by one. He even told me where I needed dental attention without looking in my mouth.

Unexpectedly, midappointment, he told me I needed to forgive my mother. With no knowledge of our past or current relationships, he blurted out those words, catching me completely off guard. For a moment I was stunned, wondering what type of telepathic powers he possessed, but he quickly moved on to the next finding. As I calmly sat there, my mind attempted to decipher what he could possibly mean by "forgive." When the scan was complete, he asked, "In your childhood, who taught you how to love?" I took a beat and then responded, "My father." He then said, "Forgive your mother for what she couldn't do that he did."

It took a few therapy sessions and intense writing sessions for me to admit what he might've been referring to. Although deep down I hadn't forgiven my mother for not fighting enough to keep the family together or raise her kids, it wasn't something I spent time thinking about. It is true that I was disappointed in her for letting go in what I had naively perceived was an easy battle, but I didn't realize I was still holding on to that twenty years later.

When my parents split, my mother moved from place to place in search of stability. Now when I look back at my parents' separation, I understand the anxiety it must've caused her: going from owning her first home to once again facing housing insecurity with no place to call her own, except this time without her children. As a child, I saw her lack of stability as a weakness, unfavorably comparing her situation to that of my father's. I often thought, "Why can't she stay in one place too long?" But as an adult with a real understanding of her history and the world she lived in, I now see that moving from place to place was all she had known, and this wasn't her fault. My mother's experience, while deeply personal, is not uncommon.

Reflecting on your own childhood, are there any financial decisions that your parents made, or continue to make, that you don't agree with? Could you benefit from having an open and honest conversation with them to better learn about their experience in that moment and the outcome they wished it would have had for you? Take some time in your journal to ponder these questions. Grasping the reasons behind our parents' financial decisions requires that we also understand how their choices may have been influenced by the economic disparities that were, and still are, prevalent in their culture or society.

I fully recognize the financial inequalities between men and women, yet I judged my mother for her struggles. She was my prime example of how to be a woman, and I saw firsthand how her fears and insecurities often led her to complain rather than demand what she deserved. A part of me wanted to see her fight in all aspects of her life. Yet, I was naive to my mother's experiences and environment. Being a Black woman working on Wall Street as an executive assistant was a big enough accomplishment in the 1990s, yet she was likely underpaid due to a combination of the color of her skin, her gender, and her lack of a college degree.

America Has a Problem

We cannot deny the difficulty minorities in the US generally face to overcome financial adversity. According to Brookings, in 2016, Black child households had just one cent for every dollar held by non-Hispanic white child households. In 2013 in the US, the average wealth (including the value of a home) of African-American families was $95,000. For Hispanics, $112,000. The average wealth of white families was $500,000 greater than it was for African-American or Hispanic families.[1] For individuals of color struggling with poverty in America, the combination of financial difficulties and an inadequate social safety net often leaves them disproportionately incapable of securing basic needs, such as food, health services, and consistent housing. And these disproportionate poverty rates and circumstances among Black communities are a direct pipeline to their overrepresentation in the homeless population.

The US faces significant economic inequality, with wealth concentrated in the hands of a small percentage of the population, and that is no fault of any individual who isn't in a position to directly impact policy. The very concept of poverty is incredibly layered. Compared to other developed nations, the US has weaker economic and health support systems, placing more financial strain on citizens for critical needs like retirement, health care, and unemployment assistance. As a result, this forces people to work longer hours to ensure these fundamental needs are met.

The allure of the American Dream often masks a reality of overexertion for many Americans. Labor as a means of survival has been ingrained in us and seeks to teach us that hard work is the only way to success. For Black Americans, our history of intense labor as a path to societal acceptance and equality has been handed down through generations. While it's commendable to be a hard-working person, most Black Americans are still underpaid, which leads to excessive stress and its consequential impacts on both mental and physical health.

I would love to find a place in the world where the color of one's skin didn't predetermine their economic destiny, but here in the US and around the world, homelessness has roots in historical and systemic inequalities that continue into the present day, affecting nearly everyone's access to adequate opportunities and resources. Consequently, this cycle of poverty and housing instability is perpetuated, creating an environment where escaping generational poverty is difficult. There's a clearly defined pattern cascaded to families: if your parents owned their home, chances are you will too; and if they were well-off, that wealth often gets handed down to the next generation. For my mother, and many like her, the challenge wasn't just a lack of wealth; it was the difficulty to make enough to get ahead and set your children up for success.

This pattern of wealth inheritance starkly contrasts the historical experiences of African Americans. With the abolition of slavery in 1865, African Americans sought to claim the lands they had toiled on involuntarily. Yet, their rightful requests were denied, while the US government simultaneously provided white settlers with free land. It was a clear message: African Americans were expected to start from nothing, regardless of the immeasurable contributions they had already made.

Similarly, the story of Native Americans is marked by a sequence of broken treaties and land seizures. The culmination of their centuries-long displacement was the Indian Removal Act of 1830, which led to the Trail of Tears and other forced relocations to reservations on infertile lands. Later, the General Allotment Act of 1887, or Dawes Act, aimed to assimilate Indigenous people by dividing communal lands into individual plots, yet this policy primarily resulted in a significant loss of tribal land to white settlers due to the sale of surplus lands. The historical impact of these policies is still evident today, with many Native American communities experiencing extremely high levels of poverty, often exceeding the rates experienced by African Americans.

The financial challenges and systemic inequities in the US have left Native American and Alaskan Native populations to face a health crisis, evident in their lower life expectancies and greater susceptibility to disease compared to other American groups.[2] Young Native American children in particular grow up in communities where schools lack resources, poverty is widespread, health care is minimal and low quality at best, and cultural misunderstandings are common. These conditions are more than individual struggles; they reflect the larger issues of systemic financial inequities that directly affect their communities, creating challenges that for many feel impossible to overcome.

> "Rarely in our life is money a place of genuine freedom, joy, or clarity, yet we routinely allow it to dictate the terms of our lives and often to be the single most important factor in the decisions we make about work, love, family, and friendship."
>
> —Lynne Twist

As I mentioned before, we often only talk about the things we feel most confident in, so it comes as no surprise that parents who excel in managing their finances are more apt to discuss it with their children. Speaking confidently about spending habits or salaries isn't merely a display of personal achievement (although some folks do brag); rather, it's usually rooted in a recognition that their insights and experiences can truly influence others. They understand that by sharing what they know, they can make a positive impact on others and change the trajectory of their lives.

Today, there is a growing trend toward incorporating financial literacy in high school curriculums, but that wasn't always the case. While the hope is for this to be accessible to all high school students, as of 2024, only twenty-five US states require high school students to complete a financial literacy course as a prerequisite for graduation.[3] This is a drastic change from the only six states that required it in 2019. I spoke to Diana Isern, founder of Fin Lit Legacies and vice principal and financial literacy educator at Brooklyn Prep High, and she shared the following:

> I want to actively change the all-too-common narrative of, "I wish I learned about investments and money

in school." The eagerness and excitement the students display when they learn how to read stock quotes and calculate compounding interest makes me inspired. I need to teach financial literacy to push the movement where all of our nation's youth take control of their financial future in the midst of so many economic uncertainties.

Our teens are perceptive in what they see around Brooklyn every day, and already have background experiences that we can leverage as entry points into the financial world. Some have started small businesses on social media. Many hold jobs and have earning potential and want to know about paycheck deductions. And all have dreams that a strong financial foundation can help them achieve. Recently, 244 students signed up for my finance course in a school of 540, which represents students' enthusiasm to invest in their futures. We must facilitate curricular spaces that empower our eager students with the tools required to make an ethical impact on our society.

Talking about money in my family was not a topic of conversation, and when my mother and I did speak about money, it was from a discouraged place. In her generation, and to a certain extent still today, many women defer to the men in the household to make the financial decisions. However, in my thirties, I went on a very deep dive into the world of personal finance. I came to understand that we have a lot more control over our circumstances than I thought growing up. So through obsessive reading of financial books and listening to podcasts, I taught myself about what I call "financial health"—budgeting, spending less, saving more, and money management. Then, as I delved more into this space, I started expanding to learn about what I consider "financial wealth"—investments, compounding, and growing generational wealth. The deep learning—and unlearning—I went through has allowed my mother and I to have great conversations about money management and wealth vehicles. Now we speak very openly about our spending, our saving, and our investing.[4]

I also asked if she learned any healthy money management tips from her mother in her childhood, despite not having the knowledge to create generational wealth. Here's what she had to say:

What I've learned is that while we can find many flaws in my parents' parenting, there's *always* something good that we find too. There's always a positive takeaway or lesson in every situation. This mindset has helped me live in a state of gratitude versus a state of blame or frustration.

1. Know how to stretch a dollar. [We had] many years of practice using twenty bucks to buy our family's meals for the week.

2. Don't depend on anyone to hold your financial future for you. Always have your own means and ways to support yourself.

3. Always have money saved. Don't spend everything on anything just to prove something to someone.

4. Give to others. Never be so greedy that you only accumulate and never give to those who need it more than you.[5]

We are sponges, constantly picking up habits in our surroundings and only wringing them out if we so choose. It was not until my midthirties that I decided to take real action and begin investing in financial stability.

In her book *The Soul of Money: Transforming Your Relationship with Money and Life*, Lynne Twist delves into our cultural attitudes toward money by examining how it is often intertwined with our ideas of success, worthiness, and happiness, and how these perceptions influence our behavior and financial relationships. Twist suggests that by reevaluating our relationship with money, we have the power to shift it from a source of anxiety and competition to a resource for personal fulfillment and positive social change.[6] A particularly striking point is the profound influence money holds over our lives, often dictating our choices if we do not consciously manage our relationship with it. A hurdle many of us face, however, is helping our loved ones realize that they do in fact have a relationship with money, and it's not just something you use.

I believe that learning through conversation and books is essential to our growth, as these resources can often provide education where parental/familial support may be lacking. I distinctly remember learning about money from Robert Kiyosaki's book *Rich Dad Poor Dad*. There weren't a ton of financial resources at my fingertips when I was a teenager, and for some reason, the Black community really gravitated toward this book. In my readings, I began to learn that money is something you don't necessarily have to always work hard for, but something that could also work for you. It helped me redefine financial freedom, seeing it as a destination that could be reached before retirement. It helped me develop a new perspective on money, debunking the traditional notion that a house or, in this case, high income alone equates to wealth, and instead highlighting the value of financial planning and investments. In reading this book, I realized that I had already picked up habits from my parents and never even considered financial planning as a necessity for success.

I started writing this chapter two weeks after finding out I was pregnant with my first child. While processing my parents' decisions, I found myself needing to reflect more on how I was choosing to show up each day. For the past year, I'd been so focused on healing my family and breaking cycles for the betterment of my nieces and nephews that I never actually considered my own future children. With the gravity of my new reality hitting me fast, I questioned how my child would be impacted by my financial choices, or even by this work.

Money is the one topic I was the most insecure talking about within my marriage. While I'd like to think I'm a great communicator, I didn't have much practice with this subject. My husband was raised by a single mother who knew how to stretch every dollar and did everything possible to educate and instill the benefits of frugality in her only son so he could grow to have an even better relationship with money than she did. She taught him about savings, homeownership, and the benefits of living below your means.

When I first met my husband, I made more than he did. I had my own apartment with a view of the NYC skyline, while he had roommates with whom he shared everything except his bedroom. I thought that meant I was so far ahead of him financially, but his savings account made mine look nonexistent. Once we got engaged, we decided to openly discuss our finances and lay everything on the table. I quickly found out that I had student loans and he didn't, I had medical debt (even prior to my consistent surgeries), and I was the one without a real retirement strategy. I was embarrassed but glad that I shared so he could know what he was getting into. Surprisingly, in talking, I found out my husband had insecurities around money as well, as he sometimes felt inadequate comparing his financial means to those of my exes. He had no idea that I admired the way he managed money. He was a man I could learn from.

Tips for Talking to Your Spouse or Partner about Finances

A huge takeaway from the many conversations I've now had with my husband is that people who financially plan will always be ahead, no matter the extravagance or perceived number of possessions. If you're interested in starting conversations with your partner or spouse around finances, here are some tips to keep in mind:

- Be open and respectful of their financial journey.
  Remember that financial education is not equal.

- Find a private setting and schedule time to discuss this so both parties can arrive at the conversation prepared.

- Create a budget together. If you will be sharing a home or possessions with a partner, you should treat it like you would managing a project with a team. Everyone needs to be on the same page about who is responsible for what.

- There's no one way to manage your finances in a partnership. Some prefer to share one account for everything, while others decide to keep things separate. The most important thing is that you are fully transparent with each other. Will you speak regularly about your spending habits, or would you prefer to track your spending some other way?

- Focus on you and your partner's strengths. My husband is much more organized than I am, and as such, he is great at paying things on time. So, he pays the bills and I send him money for them.

- Talk about your values and long-term financial goals. Allow your partner to support you or act as an accountability partner as you work to improve your credit score, increase your savings, or plan for retirement.

- Share your earnings information with each other. In order to facilitate a fair and open dialogue around money, you may find it necessary to know your partner's income. This is not a conversation you need to have at the start of a relationship, but it's certainly one you should consider as you begin building a life together.

- Be willing to teach if they're willing to grow, and vice versa. At the end of the day, you and your partner are there to help each other. Don't be afraid to share your financial knowledge or tools with your partner to help them help themselves, and try not to take things personally if your partner comes to you with knowledge you were not aware of.

Although I'm in a much more stable financial situation today, I collected over $60,000 of medical debt, which is down from the $140,000 I was initially billed, due to the help of financial aid. This debt persists not because I was uninsured but because when I finally secured an insurance plan, the company didn't cover what they categorized as "elective surgery" for endometriosis excision. Situations I considered emergencies, like breathing on only one functioning lung, weren't always covered by my plan. Consequently, the combination of unhelpful insurance, my poor financial decisions, and a system that's not designed to facilitate my financial freedom set me back even more than I already was.

In the US, the burden of medical debt is a major issue, disproportionately affecting minorities. Research shows that Black, Hispanic, and some Asian populations, when compared to white populations, appear to have lower levels of health insurance coverage, with Hispanics facing greater barriers to health insurance than any other group.[7] Reflecting on my own situation, it pains me to consider the countless people whose ability to financially plan has been hindered by medical debts. It shows yet another reason why it's so hard for people, especially people of color, to break generational patterns. Despite my knowledge and relentless efforts to advance, I was hindered by the overwhelming and uncontrollable forces of America's health system. Medical health should not impact financial health.

Regardless of where we begin, generational wealth is within our grasp if we can find the knowledge needed to advance. The concept of bettering the lives of future generations then becomes not just about passing down money but also teaching them the information that sets them up for success. You can be the one to empower your family to make informed decisions, grow their assets, and understand their rights to wealth. By openly sharing our financial successes and failures, we can equip the next generation with the tools they need to build a more secure financial future. This shift in mindset from spending to saving and investing, and our willingness to discuss what we don't know about money, is the cornerstone of building lasting wealth and financial independence. You have a right to wealth!

Questions for Yourself

Do I have a healthy relationship with money?

Like all relationships, we should take the time to occasionally evaluate our status and make sure we're in good standing. While we have free apps that can show our spending habits and help us manage our finances, I've yet to find one that holds me accountable for past decisions and the impact they have on my future plans. So, in preparation for the baby, I've started a financial progress report journal, and it's been paramount in helping me set achievable goals to overcome financial challenges.

On the first page of my progress report, I asked myself the following questions and rated myself 1–10, with 1 being the lowest score and 10 being the best possible score. I highly encourage you to ask yourself these questions and record your answers.

- How would you rate your current understanding of saving and investing?

- How confident do you feel in your planning for retirement?

- How much do you know about your family's financial history?

- How prepared are you for an emergency situation?

- How good are you at not spending more money than you earn (credit cards, loans, savings)?

Your relationship with money will also impact how you show up for others, in the same ways that it impacted how your parents showed up for you. In striving to permanently break patterns of generational financial struggle, my aim is to achieve genuine financial freedom. Here are some tips I've learned that focus on becoming financially free:

- Do not ignore your debt. It's real, and it needs to be faced and paid off. If you can't afford to pay it in full, communicate with debt collectors, inquire if there's a forgiveness program, and request a payment plan.

- Believe that you have a right to wealth and release yourself from limited beliefs.

- Acknowledge the influence that your family has had on your financial decisions and unlearn what's necessary for change.

- Ask for help. Seek guidance and support from professionals or even friends and coworkers who may be more knowledgeable or have the experience you're looking for.

- Understand that there's no final destination or number that will make you truly feel fulfilled. The more you make, the more you will want to make. Learn to be content with the amount that brings comfort in navigating everyday life.

- Save and invest.

- Teach others what you know. It feels good to give back, and it doesn't always have to be a financial contribution. Knowledge can be a person's largest asset.

Questions to Initiate Family Conversations about Finances

There are many ways and times to spark conversations about money with your family, whether via text, during a long car ride, or at the dinner table. Initiating these discussions can be as simple as sharing a personal experience or asking for advice on a financial matter. Consider using current events, financial news, or even a recent podcast or television episode to introduce the things you learned and ask questions. As with any potentially sensitive topic, be sure to set a relaxed and nonjudgmental tone to encourage your loved ones to feel safe opening up and assessing their relationship with money. Here are some open-ended questions you can ask to help your loved ones talk honestly about their relationship with money:

- What is the worst decision you've ever made with money?

- What is the best decision you've ever made with money?

- Have you ever had a job where you felt you were being paid your worth?

- What is something you wish you knew about money at a younger age?

- If you met an investor tomorrow and they were willing to back any dream or idea you had, how much would you ask for and how would you use the money?

End your conversation by sharing resources or information that you feel would be helpful toward their financial goals.

Healer's Recap

- The very concept of poverty is layered, and it is quite difficult to overcome. Don't judge yourself or others for where they start or end up.

- The allure of the American Dream often masks a reality of overexertion for many Americans. Labor as a means of survival has been ingrained in us and seeks to teach us that hard work is the only way to success. Know that this is not true; money can work for you.

- Education is key in building generational wealth.

- People who financially plan will always be ahead, no matter their possessions.

- Be honest with yourself and look for ways in which you can improve your spending habits.

- Don't depend on anyone to hold your financial future for you. Always have your own means and ways to support yourself.

- Do not ignore your debt.

- Your parents did the best they could with the tools they had.

- Regardless of where we begin, generational wealth is within our grasp if we can find the knowledge needed to advance.

Chapter Four

Limited Dreams and Aspirations

Do you question the origins of your aspirations?

It's only recently that I've begun to question where my aspirations derive from and whether or not they're manifestations of aspirations and inspirations embedded in my DNA. I'll never forget the day I released my first book. I was hosting a sold-out book signing at Barnes & Noble in Manhattan, and my mother turned and said, "I almost feel like you're living for me. You've exceeded my expectations and achieved everything I never thought I could do." Her words, though comforting, struck me like a course completion notification I'd never consciously signed up for. My mother never wanted to be a writer. What strengths did she see in me or weaknesses did she see in herself that gave her such profound pride?

To this day I'm still dissecting that comment. In an attempt to process my mother's words, I find myself wondering, *Did this idea of who I should become start with wanting to please her? Were my actions the result of the echoes of my ancestors?* My ambitions, no matter how unique they appear to me, seem intricately intertwined with the repressed legacy and unfulfilled dreams of those who came before me. While the opportunities may change for each generation, the root of our desires contain commonalities. Suddenly, with my mother's confession, I realized that her buried dreams have now flourished into new aspirations that currently rest upon my shoulders. Aspirations that perhaps only I could achieve due to my ancestors' sacrifices and the profound impact they've had on my life.

To truly understand the core of our desires, it's essential to recognize and build a relationship with our inner voice. That voice, our most authentic and unabashed thoughts, is what I like to refer to as our "first voice." It's the voice within us that has yet to be shared or influenced by the external ideas of others. For me, I hear it most when I take a shower or when I first wake up in the morning. I hear it in my moments of solitude, when I have no immediate chores or tasks to complete. My first voice typically visits me during moments of carefree stillness and isolation. By carving moments to connect with myself and tap into my inner portal, I'm able to listen to the voices I've carried silently through generations and guide myself toward a destination I may have never envisioned. Trusting this navigational pull I feel within me has been critical to my journey of deeper self-discovery.

Part of living our most fulfilled lives involves discovering our likes and dislikes while being in constant exploration of the spaces that lift our spirits. Many of us spend our entire lives trying to morph into an idealized version of ourselves, only to come up empty-handed. Instead of embracing our most authentic self, we spend countless years seeking outside validation, whether we're a young child looking for our parents' approval or an adult overthinking a social media post or how to fit in with others. In seeking external validation, we can lose sight of the things that leave us feeling truly fulfilled, failing to realize that the alignment between who we are and what we do can be a sure path to success.

The journey toward understanding myself on a deeper, more intimate level has allowed me to make room for mistakes and welcome the lessons that come hand in hand with failure. In this space, I've given myself grace and permission to fail, not because that is ever the goal but because I know I can't control every outcome. Through hard lessons, I've learned to trust myself and nurture the parts of me that need improvement, and although I have high expectations for my personal growth, I have learned that it's best to be gentle with myself.

Finding My Why

I often wonder why I aspire to master so many things and why I have this relentless drive to mark my presence across multiple industries. Is my insatiable thirst for mastery a by-product of the privilege I carry as a modern woman, empowered to be her own boss in any field she desires? Or could it be that I'm an intricately diverse individual with multiple interests who dares to chase after them all? Choosing a single career path is appealing for many, but for myself, it has always felt like more of a constraint. Even as a little girl, I found myself in a conscious state of challenging the norm, refusing to comply with the expectations of others.

Growing up, I sat around the table while my parents and their siblings complained about work and their coworkers for hours at a time. It was clear to me, even back then, that when the time came to select a job or a career, I would consider one that brought me joy. I never aspired to be the person who needed to vent or have a drink in order to unwind after each workday. While that approach may work for some, I always observed this practice as unconstructive. Without being able to fully fathom the importance of mental and physical health, I knew, at the very least, that to partake in it would be unhealthy. I wanted to break the cycle of going for the "good job," the job I need rather than the job I want.

Throughout our lives family members, friends, and even complete strangers will all share unsolicited advice on what we should be doing with ourselves. The elders in my family often suggested that I confine my ambitions to a more traditional path: go to college, find a well-paying job, work hard, and then finally find happiness in its profits during retirement. Yet, no matter what narrow path was suggested, I knew I was created to take a road less traveled. Unconsciously, I've always desired to be different, and I've never feared walking that path alone. So as I find myself navigating life in a way that feels true to my spirit and my calling, this sometimes means doing many things at once to soothe my continued curiosity.

I was born with an "I can do anything" mentality, but I'm also not ashamed to admit that I have moments of self-doubt and procrastination. If my gut tells me I'm capable, I'll go for it, but if I believe it's less doable, I'll categorize it as something I wish I could do and give it less thought, time, and effort. When pursuing a dream that I see clearly, I may second-guess myself, but more often than not, if I say I'm going to do it, then I'm going to at least try to make it happen. At some point in my childhood, I set the bar pretty high, and I've remained consistent in wanting to meet myself at my potential. I wake up each morning with a burning desire to have more, whether that's personal achievements or a prosperous career. Even that I recognize is a gift.

As a young girl, my mother had dreams of being a professional dancer. As the first in her family to pursue this type of career, she was obviously met with criticism. My grandmother saw it as nothing more than a healthy hobby to dabble in during her free time, but that's only because she hadn't known anyone to make a career out of dance, and it seemed like such a risk for her daughter to take this untraditional path. For my mother, however, she saw it as her calling. As early as the age of seven, she began studying jazz, modern dance, and ballet. Committed to her craft, as a teenager she eventually worked to cover the cost of her classes so she could take professional workshops at the infamous Alvin Ailey dance studio in Harlem. Her innate talents gave her purpose, and that purpose landed her performances at prestigious venues like Radio City and Carnegie Hall, stages that many dancers can only dream of touching. But this still didn't change my grandmother's perception of her "hobby."

My mother often tells me stories about her days as a dancer with immense pride. However, that path took an unexpected turn when she became pregnant with my brother at eighteen years old. In an instant, her dancing dreams were placed on the back burner, and the stigma of being a teen mom began to cloud her thoughts. Despite the love she had for the art, she wasn't sure if she would ever dance again. What she did know was that dance wasn't paying the bills, and as she prepared to bring life into the world, she needed to make sacrifices to offer him a better life, one with stability.

"Don't make the same mistakes your mother made," she would tell me. Yet, my mother often says that despite the outcomes, she has no regrets. I'm not sure if she says that to spare her children's feelings or if she really means it, but she's worked hard to ensure I didn't put myself in a similar situation by becoming a mother too soon. While most mothers fear their children having children too soon, for my mother, it became a generational cycle that needed to be broken. She preached that lesson to me for as long as I can remember. But my mother's concerns weren't my own. I was driven by a vision of a very different life for myself, and nothing gave me more drive than the desire to see those dreams come to life. As a young adult, I didn't desire children of my own; I just wanted to build a career where I could help children who were struggling feel seen and understood. I wanted to give to those who had even less than I did and make a difference in the world.

Though my mother was unable to pursue her dream career, she never stopped dancing. I can still vividly recall the joy in her eyes when she danced with me in our new house. It was our bonding time, and when we danced, there were no boys allowed in the room. I cherish those times as her most joyful moments. The happiness she exuded was always transferred, giving me the fuel and excitement to join her in front of the mirror and mimic her moves. With hip-hop and R&B blasting through the speakers in her bedroom, it was in those moments that she could tap into her most authentic self. I didn't understand back then just how much dance meant to her, but as I found personal interest in it, she slowly began to open up, sharing beloved memories about her own connection to the art form.

My pursuit of a professional hip-hop dance career was kismet; in discovering myself and connecting with my mother, it felt like destiny. Heavily influenced by those fond childhood memories, I went on to sign with the number one dance agency in the world, surpassing even my mother's aspirations. In my late teens and early twenties, I was fortunate to work with some of the biggest brands and musicians of my time. I booked commercials and traveled the world as a backup dancer for some of my favorite artists. When I could, I even taught dance in NYC and beyond to young aspiring dancers. Watching me live her dreams out loud made my mother so proud. That is, until I dropped out of college to do background dancing on a three-month tour.

While my mom wanted me to be a dancer, her foremost desire was for me to earn a college degree, something she was unable to do because of the timing of her pregnancies. This achievement carried significant meaning for her, especially since no one in our lineage had done it. In her eyes, dancing was merely a short-lived aspiration in the entertainment industry. For my mother, a college education meant stability. This conviction was shaped by her upbringing and reinforced by observing her peers who, with their degrees, earned higher incomes. Consequently, she desired the same opportunity for her children, hoping to give us a fair chance at achieving stability and success.

In 2000, only 6.4 percent of Black adults had an associate degree, while 10.4 percent obtained a bachelor's degree.[1] These statistics, however, don't reflect African Americans' interest in attending and finishing school. If college was affordable for all, I think it's safe to assume that these numbers would look drastically different. Far more than a mere academic achievement, a college degree for many within the Black community represents a collective victory against systemic educational barriers. Historically, obtaining a degree has meant more than just personal success; it's an act of reclaiming a right that was once denied. With a formal education, we are given the tools to break cycles of poverty, challenge long-standing stereotypes, and lay the foundation for the prosperity of future generations. It's our American Dream. But for many, it is also often an unaffordable one.

My parents made it clear that after high school, I needed to go to college, regardless of whether I knew what I wanted to study or not. Despite my lack of surety, my parents believed that gaining a college education was essential to my success. Dance felt like a personal achievement, but college felt like a communal goal. I knew that enrolling would signify generational resilience and provide my family with a profound sense of pride, even if I didn't finish. And so I went, and so did my brother, but neither of us had the financial means to complete our degrees in the end. I was forced to drop out and return much later when I was financially independent and able to cover my own tuition.

The more we talk to people, the more we understand their intentions. There were times my elders tried to instill fear in me when they discovered I'd considered a path that didn't align with what made them most comfortable. My mother projected her insecurities onto me, something I'm sure she was taught by generations before her. When parents do this, they often believe that instilling a sense of caution or awareness of life's imminent challenges will prepare you for the complexities of the world. However, this projection often stems from their experiences, anxieties, or unfulfilled aspirations. Even with the best intentions, they might unconsciously transfer those feelings of doubt onto you. My advice: try to gain an understanding of their why, acknowledge whether or not their input comes from a place of deep love, but don't let it halt your plans.

I've always listened to the advice my parents have given me, but it's also been important for me to recognize where their dreams end and mine begin. On the day I left for Los Angeles to start college, my father was so disappointed in my decision to move cross country he didn't even get out of bed to give me a hug goodbye. I don't know if he was frustrated or heartbroken, but he made it clear all summer that he wanted me to stay and enroll in community college. When I chose to go against his wishes, I suspect he still thought I would reconsider. After all, he couldn't have imagined his daughter could be just as stubborn as him.

I'm the first generation in my family to have the option to self-educate, start and scale a business, reach anyone in the world via the internet, choose healing through professional resources, and make happiness a priority—something I don't want to take for granted. On my winding path of self-discovery, I've found myself taking leaps of faith into unfamiliar territories and learning skills that were foreign to my parents as well as my ancestors. In an effort to stay true to my needs, after dropping out of college, I briefly ventured into songwriting. I knew I wasn't the greatest vocalist, but my pen game was strong, and I could effortlessly write catchy hooks and melodies. Though my songwriting endeavors were short-lived, it did land me a placement on a Grammy Award–winning album. This grand achievement was one that I know my ancestors could have never imagined possible. Though I have yet to discover an ancestor with a love or propensity for singing or songwriting, I want to believe that this gift was passed down to me by one of them.

In many countries around the world, it's true that you can be virtually anything you want to be. My friend in social advocacy, Tiffany Loftin, is a full-time activist, a career that allows her to stand in her truth and fight on the front lines for communities and campaigns that advocate for justice and equality, all while earning an income. At times, Tiffany has held full-time jobs, such as her role as the national director of the NAACP Youth & College Division, and at other times, she's volunteered for charitable causes. We had a recent conversation, and she shared some of the reservations her family has had about her career choice:

> My family wanted me to be a lawyer; they wanted me
> to make money and fight for people. I guess this is
> me doing the same thing. It wasn't until my first year
> of college when the University of California Regents
> increased our tuition 36 percent that I started to dis-
> cover ways students could work together to create
> change. I'll never forget how excited I was after pro-
> testing the Regents. I called my mother to tell her that
> I was becoming a leader and demonstrating my power
> with my fellow students, and my mother was so scared
> for me. Not only because she financially was not able
> to support me if something did happen, but because
> I told her I was facing the police head-on to fight for
> higher education.
>
> I remember telling my uncle and my dad about my
> trip to Palestine on a racial justice delegation . . . my father
> insisted that he go with me. I told him that we had gone
> through checkpoints and faced Israeli soldiers head-on
> about the genocide and racial apartheid happening there,

and he was terrified for my safety. I kind of learned to stop sharing moments of protest with my family; their biggest fear is that I will get arrested. But I read Nelson Mandela's autobiography, and he spent most of his life in prison for what he believed in. He had to give up some of the most important memories and moments that anyone can experience in life—watching his children grow up, watching them have grandchildren, and unfortunately watching some of them pass away before him. I don't want to stress my (biological) family out, but my community in movement has become my family. The folks I protest with, those I lock arms with, those I cry with, and those I march with. I didn't know it could be a career. Honestly it has been my heart's work.

I'm also inspired by my trip to Ghana that I took with the NAACP a few years back for the year of the return. When we went to the slave castles, it was overbearing, and I started to break down and cry. One of the tour guides, whose name was Justice, grabbed me before I hit the floor and gave me a hug. I don't know anything about my ancestors connected to the continent but what Justice told me will change my life forever. He said to me, "I know this is painful, but you must understand that your ancestors are celebrating and rejoicing because you completed the journey to bring them home." And in that moment my life had been changed forever. I carry my ancestors with me wherever I go, whatever I do, and whatever I am fighting for. I am contributing to the legacy of everyone who has come before me. And as Brittany Packnett always says, "I'm working to be a good ancestor."

Before Tiffany and after, there have been many activists, but few have been able to accomplish what she has in making it her full-time career, being wholeheartedly immersed in her passion and breaking free from limiting beliefs—and in many ways her family's fears.

In 2011, my mother introduced me to the notion of helping children in foster care acquire healthy coping skills. Originally intended as a passion project built around my day job, my work with the Precious Dreams Foundation quickly transitioned into a full-time endeavor. My mother never imagined I would start a nonprofit, create a salary, hire a team, expand across the nation, and turn the idea into a vehicle to create a lasting legacy. And while I knew it was possible to do so, she simply hadn't known any other Black woman who accomplished such a thing, so her mind didn't allow her to envision it.

The challenging aspect of selecting a full-time career path is assessing if it allows you to earn a sustainable living, grow and feel fulfilled, or both. When I started the Precious Dreams Foundation, I wasn't taking a grand leap of faith. I had a secure job, and I stayed there until I was confident I could transition successfully. It's also important to know that if your desires are driven by simple basic needs and you don't have a "dream job" in sight, that's completely normal. American psychologist Abraham Maslow's hierarchy of needs suggests that a person must fulfill their basic needs before they can consider acting on more advanced desires. Maslow explained that humans have an inborn desire to be self-actualized, but first they must ensure their needs for food, safety, love, and self-esteem are met. The five levels of Maslow's hierarchy of needs (often viewed as a pyramid), ranked from the bottom to the top, are:

- **PSYCHOLOGICAL:** All essential needs for human survival. This includes having clean water, fresh air, shelter, food, and sleep. Without these basic needs, it's extremely challenging for one to focus on other desires.

- **SECURITY AND SAFETY:** This includes financial health, overall wellness, and employment.

- **SOCIAL:** Everyone wants to do life with others, regardless of the guards they may put up or the comfort they may feel in their lonely hours. Our social needs are fulfilled by friendships, family relationships, social groups, and generally connecting with others.

- **ESTEEM:** If the first three levels are met, people will naturally seek respect and appreciation from others, both of which can build their self-esteem.

- **SELF-ACTUALIZATION:** This last need concerns personal growth and development and can only be realized once you get to a point where you're less driven by the opinions of others. With all needs met, people are more easily able to visualize themselves as their best selves.[2]

Keeping these innate needs in mind, set goals and expectations that address which aspect of the hierarchy is most pressing to you right now, and perhaps you'll be able to release some of the common pressures that may have been placed on you from everyone around you—the pressures to provide, do something purposeful, or make others proud. Each of these pressures can be felt at once, and all are capable of causing crippling anxiety and indecisiveness if they're not managed properly.

The Pressure to Provide

One of the most fundamental pressures adults face in their careers is the need to provide for themselves or their families. This pressure encompasses all of our basic needs, like food, shelter, and health care, and extends to our future security in the form of savings and retirement plans. These pressures can become overwhelming, especially when they're experienced in an unpredictable economy or in industries with frequent job insecurity. Understandably, this is why many parents prefer that their children prioritize jobs that have a proven track record of financial stability over those that might be riskier and only fulfill personal passions or talents. On the other hand, constant financial worry can lead to us devoting long hours to our jobs just to keep our heads above water, which in turn can lead to us experiencing burnout and the overwhelming feeling of being trapped in a career chosen more out of necessity than desire.

It should be noted that this pressure can look different over generations, despite many of the similarities we endure. What becomes clear is that even with state or government assistance, no one is going to care for you unless you care for yourself. To bring your dreams to fruition, you must show up and work diligently toward them. Many of us learn this, sometimes the hard way, as young adults when we finally venture into the world on our own. It's a timeless notion that resonates across eras and circumstances, reminding us that our individual effort matters and we are responsible for the journey of our life and career.

The Pressure to Do Something Purposeful

Part of living our most fulfilled lives involves the quest to find purpose-driven work, an opportunity that wasn't always given to our ancestors. In contrast to the pressure to provide, here there is an idealistic pressure to pursue one's dreams, which stems from a societal narrative that encourages us to find our "true calling" or passion and turn it into a career. The idea is well-intended but can cause extreme anxiety for many who lack the guidance or resources to make this a reality. This pursuit can often involve unavoidable risks, whether financial, personal, or social, and can lead to a constant internal struggle between following a dream and choosing a more stable and secure career path. For those who choose the "safer" path (because let's be real, no job is guaranteed), it can cause a sense of unfulfillment or regret for not chasing their true passions. For others, it can stir up feelings of insecurity or aimlessness from simply not being able to pinpoint what their dreams actually are.

As soon as we graduate from high school, we are often tasked with deciding who we aspire to be, all while removing ourselves from an environment where people have always told us how we should be. Our time in solitude, at this point, may have been limited, and our voice, the one that tells us what we really want, may not even be recognizable. This struggle often reflects the broader challenge of balancing societal norms and personal desires in the pursuit of a satisfying life.

The Pressure to Make Others Proud

Lastly, there's the pressure to make others proud, which can be particularly intense in cultures that place high value on certain professions or see career success as a measure of overall worth as a human being. The desire to earn the respect and admiration of family, friends, and society as a whole can often lead individuals to pursue careers that align more with external expectations than with their own interests or abilities. In doing so, individuals undertake professions they're not passionate about or are unsuitable for, resulting in dissatisfaction and a lack of authentic self-expression in their work.

Each of these pressures can create a sense of overall indecisiveness. The fear of not making enough money, the worry of not fulfilling one's potential, and the anxiety of possibly disappointing those you love most can paralyze one's decision-making and lead to a career path that's driven more by fear than aspiration. Balancing these pressures requires introspection, a clear understanding of one's priorities, and often the courage to make difficult choices that align with one's true values and desires regardless of what others may say.

Questions for Yourself

What pressures do I put on myself when it comes to my career?

Pressure can produce anxiety and stress, which can leave many people feeling stagnant or unable to make sound decisions. To find your way through external pressures, you must decide what the pressures you're feeling mean to you and how you'd like to respond to them. For me personally, the pressure to make great money has always weighed on me the most, wanting to break the cycle of just getting by. But after I became content with my salary, I began to develop a reliance on achievement in order to feel good. These pressures I set for myself came with annual financial goals, expectations for growth, and a constant desire to reach the next pinnacle. Having these self-inflicted pressures has made it challenging for me to walk with a sense of gratitude and find happiness in each day, whether it was uneventful or rewarding. At the same time, though, I have to keep in mind that these are pressures I'm putting on myself, so it's important that I continually question whether or not they're fair, treating them with the level of reflection and consideration I would for outside pressures.

According to a 2022 study published by Gallup, 60 percent of people reported being emotionally detached at work, and 19 percent identified as being miserable.[3] Your present reality and your future self hinge upon the steps you take to achieve personal fulfillment, and this requires that you check the pressures that are impacting your ability to make the next move. To get some additional guidance on how we all can show up each day and do what we love despite societal and familial pressures, I sat down with author and multidisciplinary healer Devi Brown, who shared some eye-opening questions that I believe everyone should contemplate:

> In primordial sound meditation, there are four questions that we always work with, and it's such a great starting place. You're meant to ask these questions and not try to quantify them with any answers because you just don't know the answers yet. So it's really just setting into your awareness.
>
> One of the first questions that we ask in meditation is, "Who am I?" And you don't try to fill that with the "I'm this. I'm strong. I'm motivated. I'm funny." You just leave it—"Who am I?"
>
> Next ask, "What do I really want? What do I really want right now?" You don't need to make your twenty-year plan. I don't even think young people should be focused on really being too tied to a five-year plan. I think those are really outdated methods of a work system that doesn't exist anymore. But what do I really want?

Then ask, "What am I grateful for?" And that begins to show you how you experience gratitude. It shows you an opening to receive and amplifies your ability to reach out and ask for help if you need it.

And the final question is "What's my purpose?" In meditation, we use the word dharma, which is a similar translation in Sanskrit, but it means a little bit more than purpose. It's the totality of who you are, including your experiences, your skills, your gifts, and the way you're meant to serve the world. So when we ask, "What is my purpose?" it's from a lens of "How am I meant to serve?" Not "How am I meant to be seen?" but "How am I meant to serve?"

On a spiritual level, those are always four questions that are wonderful to work with. More on the non-spiritual level, I'd say begin to get clear on what your natural curiosities are. Ask God how you're designed to be used. Notice how God uses you. I would also more specifically ask a question I always have clients use, which is, "God, Spirit, universe"—however we want to word that—"please show me the truth of who I am. Show me how I can serve." I think it is one of the most powerful activating things we can say out loud, especially when you're at such a beginner's start that there really is no foundation.

Get in touch with those questions where you'll begin to really accept and have reverence for your own story and the way your unique brain works and sees the world. When we don't take the time to do that, that's when we sit and compare, and we notice how everyone else flows and moves.[4]

If you're in a place of transition in your career or if you're trying to understand exactly what career is meant for you, begin to differentiate between what you're capable of and what the rest of the world is doing. One helpful suggestion in your quest to get to know yourself is to take an online personality test like Enneagram or 16 Personalities. These tests can provide invaluable insights about your behavior, your strengths and weaknesses, and how others may perceive you.

Your purpose will not reveal itself overnight, nor will it remain the same throughout your life, so be patient with yourself. If in moments of meditation, grounding, or during a long shower, your first voice tells you to honor your family's advice, then do just that. But if it doesn't, that's okay too. Your career is a decision that demands so much of your time and attention each day, and if you choose to be something new tomorrow or next year, that's fine. Allow room for flexibility in your decisions so you don't live with regrets.

Five Ways to Cope with External Pressure

To help you navigate external pressures that may be preventing you from living in your truth and authenticity, here are a few ways you can begin to cope and cultivate a life that brings you peace and joy, regardless of how it may be perceived by others.

1. Seek Support

- Surround yourself with people who genuinely understand and appreciate your interests and ambitions. This could be friends, mentors, or colleagues.

- Join online or in-person communities or clubs where you can share your experiences and gain insights from others.

- Engage with people who leave you feeling inspired. It's important to be among those who motivate and uplift you and validate your desires.

2. Go to Therapy

- Professional counseling can help you manage the stress or pressure you're experiencing from family, work, or the decisions around either.

- In a safe space, learn coping strategies for your challenges and anxieties.

- Explore different types of therapy and therapists until you find what's best for you.

- Note: Therapy is your friend, but it is not your career coach. Don't go into your sessions with any expectations that your therapist will have all the answers you're seeking.

3. Make a Safe Choice

- A safe career choice is not to be confused with an easy one or a "safe" job. Rather, it's the ability to choose a path that won't cause you or anyone else physical, mental, or emotional harm or danger.

- Evaluate your options in terms of job security, personal fulfillment, and opportunities for growth. Take note of which qualities are most important to you and act accordingly.

- Don't be afraid to make a sensible choice if it helps you maintain a stable foundation for your future goals. It's not about what other people think; it's about what makes the most sense for you. You can always switch to something a little riskier once you feel more stable.

4. Communicate with Others

- Try discussing your interests openly with your family. Communication is crucial in being understood at home and out in the world. Just remember that even if you share honestly and clearly, your family may still disagree. Take comfort in the fact that you've made an effort and expressed your reasoning.

- Establish boundaries and express the desire for support and understanding from your loved ones.

- Practice active listening when others express their concerns and try to foster mutual understanding and respect for each other's perspectives. After all, respect goes both ways.

5. Cultivate Self-Awareness

- Find time for solitude or engage in mindfulness practices, such as meditation, yoga, or deep breathing exercises, to maintain a clear and focused mind.

- In a journal or in your notes, create a list of personal goals that reflect your interests and values. These should be separate from external expectations.

- Explore! Find time to engage in activities that truly interest you, even if they don't align with your current career or what others expect from you. Continuously try new things, especially those things you are increasingly curious about. These thoughts are arising for a reason.

Although I'm very different from my mother, I carry so many of her attributes within me, and for that I have a lot of pride. While I know I innately have my own skills and ideas, I was curious to learn whether or not my mother felt the sum of my character could be credited back to our lineage, perhaps those whom I haven't even met. Out of pure curiosity, I decided to make up the following questions and ask them rapid-fire just to see what she would say. I also asked myself the same questions. It was interesting to see where we each gave credit. I encourage you to try this with your loved ones to determine how much of your personality and characteristics were passed down or picked up from others along the way.

ME: Personality-wise, who would you say I'm most similar to in the family?

MOM: Me.

MY THOUGHTS: My father's aunt Genny. I never had the chance to meet my grandfather on my paternal side, but I grew up in close proximity to his sister Genny. She was an Aries like me, and I admired her caretaking and independent traits so much. I would study her carefully and try to learn how to show up for others with grace and confidence like she did.

ME: Where do I get my activist spirit/desire to change the world?

MOM: Me.

MY THOUGHTS: My grandfather on my father's side. He stood up to his parents by marrying outside of his race and left everything he'd ever known in the South to move to the North to give his family a better chance at freedom and social justice. Perhaps the desire comes from my mother, but the ability to act may come from someone else. Interestingly, while it was her idea to start the foundation, I took the idea and brought it to life. So I will be forever grateful for my mother for sparking the change that I'm able to make through Precious Dreams Foundation.

ME: Where do I get my interest in writing?

MOM: I'm not sure.

MY THOUGHTS: I'll give myself the credit here. Growing up, I didn't see my parents write much, although it was my dad's preferred form of communication.

ME: Where do I get my entrepreneurial spirit?

MOM: Your great-grandparents on my side. They sold food out of their kitchen, straight to the community. Back then it was hard to own your own restaurant, but this was their way of creating their own source of income.

MY THOUGHTS: My great-grandparents on both sides. Both of my great-grandparents cooked for their communities and sold plates of food.

ME: Where do I get my desire to help others?

MOM: Definitely from me and Grandma Geri.

MY THOUGHTS: Both of my parents. I grew up watching my mother treat the world with kindness. I saw my father show up for people in need. He would go shovel snow for free or fix things that broke in our neighbors' homes just to be helpful. On any given day, if my father was in the backyard, you could hear one of the elderly neighbors calling his name out their window. That really stuck with me.

ME: I am absolutely an empath. Where do you think I get that from?

MOM: Definitely me.

MY THOUGHTS: My mother without a doubt.

ME: Where do I get my go-getter/take-charge attitude?

MOM: Combination of me and your dad.

MY THOUGHTS: Mostly my father. My mother will move fast to achieve anything she sets her mind to, but my father will do the same with an eagerness to learn new things, get uncomfortable, and risk failure.

Developing a closer relationship with my mother has notably helped me embrace the parts of myself that need healing while celebrating my accomplishments she may have influenced. Over the years, the most impactful lessons I've learned from her were not from things she said but the way she carried herself amidst some of life's greatest challenges. Through her, I've learned compassion, altruism, kindness, and resilience. Our relationship has also taught me how to have uncomfortable but necessary conversations and how to honor my needs. So much of who I am today is because my mother was willing to break the cycle of generational silence or at least work at showing me how to do it myself. While I'm grateful for her wisdom, I also recognize that my mother's family is only half of mine.

I now have the fuel to spark conversations with my other side, the Russells. I've learned just how much I could gain from getting uncomfortable, and it has helped me build the courage for future conversations.

Ways to Spark Conversations about the Road You Wish to Take

There is no right or wrong path to take in life. Many times it's hard for our families to wrap their minds around who we've chosen to be despite who they used to know or hoped we would become.

- REMEMBER THAT CONNECTION IS KEY: When preparing to have a conversation about your aspirations, aim to connect with family members in the least distracting environment possible. It's easier to open up when you have someone's full attention. Some suggested locations include talking over a meal at a restaurant, in a quiet home, or on a walk or hike.

- INVITE YOUR FAMILY TO YOUR WORK WORLD: Share stories and showcase your work or passion. If possible, bring your loved ones to see where you work, create, or build. Allowing them to see you in your career firsthand gives them insight into how you show up outside of the family dynamic.

- **DISRUPT UNWANTED DIALOGUE RESPECTFULLY:** When you find yourself on the receiving end of words that do not affirm the destiny you wish for yourself, speak up. Let your family know that while you will consider their advice, your desire to make your own decisions is important as well. Then redirect the conversation by changing the topic or thanking them for their input.

- **TAKE PRIDE IN YOUR WORK:** Success speaks louder than words. Share your achievements, promotions, or work feedback with your loved ones. When you're happy and you're great at what you do, people who genuinely have your best interest in mind will support you.

Healer's Recap

- Do soul-filling work; your ancestors will be proud of your success no matter which path you choose.

- Learn what your inner voice sounds like, then build a relationship of trust with yourself. In a world full of bias and discrimination, we must be confident in what we choose to do and prioritize success over survival.

- Believe that you will find your tribe—in life, in your personal interests, and in your career field.

- Take time to reflect on what you genuinely enjoy doing and what you are good at. You may have strengths in areas you've never considered.

- Remain flexible. Understand that your path is constantly being created.

- Pay attention to your mental health as you embark on your career journey. What you do for a living will have an impact on how you feel each day.

- Whenever you are able, go for the job you want, not the job you need.

- Meditate and you will find yourself! At any point of the day, you can close your eyes, focus on your breath, and tap the mind to either be still or ponder certain thoughts.

- There is no right path. Do it scared!

Part Two

My Father's Silence

Chapter Five

Navigating Racism

Have you thought about the ways that adverse experiences or trauma forced your parents to hide parts of themselves or grow up too fast?

I take pride in being a Black woman and knowing the challenges my family has overcome, but when I was a little girl, I wanted everyone to know that I was part white, part Black, and part Puerto Rican. I felt that sharing all of those things, despite what people could see, would allow me to gain acceptance from others. My ignorance toward Black suffering and the experience of my ancestors allowed me to form the belief that I needed to show people I belonged. Reflecting on it now, I'm not sure where that mindset came from, whether it was passed down from one of my parents or something I saw other kids doing.

Wallace Russell Sr.

Over the years, my father, Wallace Russell Sr., and I have managed to build a relationship of deep affinity, even in the absence of deep, meaningful conversations. As a child, I became an observant student of my father's world; I learned his favorite hobbies, colors, sports teams, and foods. I can tell you his favorite melodies, and when I close my eyes, I can hear him singing doo-wops in the same way I can still vividly hear his mother, my grandmother Rose, sing gospel songs as she waxed the stove clean. Nonverbal communication wasn't my preference as a child, but growing up with a father who expressed himself through acts of kindness taught me that words aren't always necessary to truly understand someone. This lesson, passed down by my father, is one of the most valuable I've ever acquired.

I've always been able to sense his mood or when he doesn't want to be bothered. This heightened sensitivity became a vital skill for navigating daily life within our home. My father was a man of few words when engaging with me, but when he chose to speak with others, you could hear him from a mile away. He often carried conversations with his upbeat personality and affinity for being selectively open with topics he enjoyed, like competitive sports and music. Inside the house, he carried a different energy, and he rarely spoke with my brother and me about the past unless I prodded him. To this day, he isn't as forthcoming as my mother. At a young age, it taught me to read the room (or between the lines) and hold space for the unspoken language of others' mental and emotional states.

My father grew up in Jamaica, Queens, with a single mother and his three siblings. He was a natural-born leader and helped my grandmother take care of the house, working as young as twelve years old. To those who know him best, he'll always be the tough kid with a big smile. Though he didn't do it often, when he did smile, you'd instantly see the light from his spirit emanate from within him. Even today, as he grows older, I can picture him as a child, yearning for life's simple joys, undeterred by the harsh realities around him. I imagine him much like myself, observing his strong parent working hard to keep the house from falling, and wondering what was going on in his mother's busy mind.

In my quest for healing, I've chosen to adopt a direct approach in my questioning of others, though I'm aware that this approach isn't preferred by all. To heal with or through my father, I recognized that I first needed to become more curious about how to gently approach uncomfortable conversations with the ones I seek to know most. On this journey, I've learned that leaning more heavily on conversations with those who are more comfortable sharing their story is integral in gaining the answers I seek about him. At the age of sixty-six, I can't imagine that my father is necessarily open to taking a new approach to healing, but you never know!

Do you ever wonder how your parents' childhoods shaped or changed who they became? This is something I've been curious about since I was a young girl. When my father was impatient or too stressed to be bothered, I often wondered if his mother was that way with him and his siblings. I wondered what traits were carried over, and I wondered what made him such an apparent tough guy. Each time I was around my grandmother Rose, she always held a straight face unless she was watching her stories, sitting on a porch, or singing gospel songs. I often wondered about her parenting style. I wondered if my father had a supportive space or trusted individual he could share his emotions with.

If you couldn't tell by now, I was a curious kid, and I've wanted to learn about my familial story for as long as I can remember. I often turned to the women in my family to gain the answers I was in search of about my father, engaging in conversations with my great-aunt Genny or asking my mother questions, as I knew my mother had known my father since they were children. Like a pint-sized detective, I hoped to gather the pieces to the puzzle that encompassed his life to better understand who he was and feel closer to the man who contributed so much to who I'd one day become.

Now as an adult, my curiosity about my father has only grown. A man of many layers and a lot of mystery. So much of me wants to ask him, "What contributed to you becoming the man you are today? What were your toughest battles? What are your emotional wounds?" But will I get the answers I'm seeking? Maybe not. If I were to ask these questions directly, he would most likely respond with something like, "Find something better to do with your time, Cole!" which is a typical response to any topic he doesn't want to engage with. And, with that, the conversation would come to an abrupt end. When I was growing up, my father didn't have time for my questions, so I just added them to a mental list that could truly fill the pages of an entire book. These kinds of interactions left me with an unquenchable thirst for some kind of insight into the depths I knew he possessed, depths that were perhaps the result of deep-seated childhood wounds.

Emotional Wounds

Emotional wounds are the negative emotional impacts many of us are left with when we experience traumatic events that instill fear within us. Almost everyone has experienced emotional wounds at some point in their lives. Unlike a painful memory, an emotional wound stems from harsh criticism, micromanagement by those in an authoritative position, being overlooked or neglected, and feeling undervalued or unworthy as a human. Our brains treat emotional pain similarly to that of physical pain. Whether we stumble and hurt our arm or someone triggers our emotions, our brains respond to this unpleasant experience by releasing the same chemicals that act as painkillers to support us as we cope. Just like the scrapes on our knees, emotional wounds from our childhood can leave marks too.

As we experience life, we naturally develop defense mechanisms that aim to protect us from encountering those same emotional wounds. According to holistic therapist Shadya Karawi Name, whether our mechanisms are healthy or not, what we have in common is that they all stem from the following:

- **FEAR OF ABANDONMENT:** Often developed between newborn and three years old, this stems from a child feeling intense loneliness, possibly due to an absent parent or significant emotional disconnect, particularly with the parent of the opposite sex. As a result, this wound leads to a defense mechanism of dependence, resulting in emotional reliance on those outside of themselves, like partners and close associates.

- **FEAR OF REJECTION:** This wound develops during the first year of life, primarily with the same-sex parent, stemming from feelings of nonacceptance or inadequate care due to various reasons. An example of this can be a depressed parent who isolates themselves or simply walks away from their responsibilities. As a result, this can lead to the child developing a tendency toward isolation or extreme physical and emotional detachment from relationships in adulthood. Throughout my adulthood, I've encountered many people who isolate themselves or self-sabotage relationships when they think someone is about to push them away.

- **FEAR OF BETRAYAL:** Developed between ages two and four, this fear is rooted in a child's feeling of being betrayed or disappointed by their caregiver, which, in turn, leads to a need for control and a difficulty in trusting others. An example of how this may manifest in adulthood is someone who often says they don't need anyone or prefers not to have friends, but deep down they do.

- **FEAR OF HUMILIATION:** This wound, formed between ages one and three, is marked by frustrated pleasure experiences and leads to self-sacrificing behaviors and a fear of emotional overwhelm. This is often seen in those who are people-pleasers or shut down in overwhelming situations.

- **FEAR OF INJUSTICE:** This wound forms between ages four and six as a result of suppressed individuality and/or distance from a same-sex parent, which results in rigidity and a pursuit of emotional perfection. In adolescence and adulthood, this can manifest as someone who is overly consumed with getting perfect grades and endlessly strives to live in a pain- and mistake-free world, often to their detriment.[1]

Fear is the common enemy in all of these scenarios. Shadya shares, "If you can identify what is your predominant wound and the mechanism that you use [to soothe it], you can transform your life completely and free yourself from the need to reproduce experiences that no longer fulfill a purpose of love in your life. You begin to understand that each experience you have lived has had a reason for being and that you no longer need to continue acting in the same way. So, little by little, you are peeling more layers and you are getting closer to connecting with your pure essence."[2]

Knowing how much my father has overcome, I'm grateful the world can still see the pure essence of who he is when he smiles or laughs out loud. I see it when he plays with his grandchildren and when he talks about his beloved basketball team, the New York Knicks. I see it in the spaces where he feels completely safe and is able to let his guard down. As someone who's never been to therapy, I wonder if he even believes he carries any childhood wounds or recognizes how his past traumas impact the way he shows up in the present.

So, how can we discover our parents' emotional wounds without asking? To go beneath my father's layers, I needed to find out what my father's childhood trauma and experiences were like. What I already knew was that at age five or six he lost his father to senseless violence. Based on my understanding of mental health and psychological scars, I could guess this perhaps triggered both the fear of abandonment and fear of injustice within him. While I don't know the details of what home life was like after my grandfather's passing, from conversations with his siblings, I do know of additional trauma that my family endured around that time, one they aren't embarrassed to speak about and one that stemmed from how they were treated as children because of the color of their skin.

My grandparents moved North to give their children a better life that was less restricted by the lack of work and educational opportunities presented to Black folks in the South. But no matter how far they ventured, they couldn't hide from racist ideals. One story I'll never forget is overhearing my father talk about being chased by white children while having rocks thrown at him and his siblings on their way to school just for being Black. He didn't reflect on it with a sense of shame but more so as a challenge he overcame. I remembered butting in to ask if he threw rocks back, and he quickly answered no with no further explanation. He shared this story with a sense of calmness, perhaps because he saw that treatment as a regular part of life, a reality that, while still bad, was better than that of his ancestors.

One of the hallmarks of being a Black parent in America is teaching your children how to respond to racism. Parents do this preventative work with the certainty and fear that at some point their child will be bullied, discriminated against, or wrongfully accused of something because of the color of their skin. So we teach our kids how to manage their emotions in the moment and suppress any boiling desire to respond with the same harmful energy. We've come to accept that unfair treatment is our norm, and if we don't prepare our children for it, it can result in severe punishment or death.

Race-Related Trauma Wounds

Everything my father and those who came before him have experienced has in some way had a generational impact on me and my brother. While I can only speculate what my father's emotional wounds may be, what I know for sure is that while growing up in the 1960s, he experienced his share of racism. Growing up as a mixed-race individual, especially during the era my father did, likely presented challenges I can't even fathom, but I was determined to learn. To begin, I needed to learn about the impact of racial trauma on his development through a mix of research and conversations. I intended to learn more about the traits my father has passed down to me, like our innate ability to fight for everyone we love and exert tremendous efforts to help those who need our assistance. There's no doubt in my mind that trauma impacts the roles we play in society.

When you look at the data, you cannot deny that racism exists. According to an AP News article, Black adolescents in America experience, on average, five forms of racial discrimination per day.[3] Additionally, studies by the CDC show that racism is detrimental to the physical health of Black people, regardless of age, gender, or economic status. With symptoms like chronic stress, cardiovascular issues, inflammatory diseases, and even cancer,[4] racism has the ability to change the trajectory of Black lives, no matter how we or others downplay it or ignore its history. Experts believe that the accumulation of stress from lifelong exposure to both structural and interpersonal racism plays a significant role in these adverse health outcomes. In the book *Inflamed: Deep Medicine and the Anatomy of Injustice* authors Rupa Marya and Raj Patel point out the very obvious impact of systemic racism, which ultimately impacts everything from the air we breathe to our grocery options and the racial violence we are exposed to. They emphasize that these factors, rooted in systemic injustice, contribute significantly to the influx of medical illnesses, both physical and mental, in marginalized communities.[5] Despite this, the long-term impacts of racism remain less explored. Understanding both the immediate and enduring repercussions of racial discrimination is crucial in creating effective and timely interventions as well as support systems tailored to the unique needs of this community.

Slavery—and the debilitating mental and physical conditions that came along with it—was a harsh life sentence for close to thirteen generations of Black Americans. When it was abolished in 1865, the absence of guidance, education, and racial equality left about 3.9 million African Americans grappling with life after "freedom." This newfound liberty enabled a new generation to earn an income in pursuit of financial independence, acquire an education, own property, and forge a new path toward wealth that was capable of benefiting future generations to come. However, such progression also introduced countless limitations, like prevailing segregation laws, discriminatory practices in employment and academia, and systemic barriers in property ownership that severely restricted the advancements many Black folks were determined to achieve. Reflecting on this period, it seems unrealistic to expect that they could rapidly climb the economic ladder within a single generation, or even several, given the pervasive inequalities they faced.

My father's roots trace back to Estill, South Carolina, a town with a population of 2,040 and a median income of $19,454 in 2020.

My brother, my parents, and I spent every summer there before the divorce. I looked forward to stopping to purchase boiled peanuts along the route and then sitting for hours watching fireflies from the porch with the elders once we arrived. For fun, my brother and I would run from house to house playing games while bugging our great-aunts and uncles to let our cousins come out and play.

In Estill, there is a long stretch of unpaved road that my family refers to as the Russell plantation. On this particular road, my family occupied the homes as far as one could see, and so, in my young mind, it felt like we owned the town. In my innocence, I never could have imagined what took place on that land only generations before me. But in doing research on Estill, I came across Bostick Plantation.[6] What a coincidence that a Bostick Plantation existed in this very small town, and I still have cousins who carry that name today. Digging for information, I called my younger cousin Earl, who carries this last name, and asked if he knew anything about it. I've never met Earl, but we connected through social media and he speaks to my father often. Only a recent college graduate, Earl admitted that he didn't know. "Ask my older sister; she knows way more than I do." Turning to yet another cousin I had never met, I sent a direct message to his sister, and she asked me to call.

Nervously, I made small talk and then asked, "Are you familiar with the Bostick Plantation?" Apparently her brother gave her the heads up that I would be reaching out, so she was already prepared with an answer.

"Our grandmother and our mother never said anything about a plantation. I don't know anything about that."

"Well, there's a chance that Bostick is a slave name that was passed on from a master," I said. I know she must've thought to herself, *Why is this girl calling me about this?* She probably thought I was crazy. Here I was, an apparent stranger in search of the roots of our last names, asking questions that could trigger someone like a fresh wound, but I figured that, perhaps like me, she too would be curious or open to learning more about her past. Turns out she wasn't. She quickly changed the topic, and instead we began to discuss her desire to feel closer to family and how much it meant for her to be in touch with those who were putting in effort.

What I learned from that conversation is that sometimes it's not that someone isn't open or curious about the past; it's that they simply aren't interested, and that's okay. They haven't processed any potential negative impacts to their family's deep history, and they're fine with focusing on the present. For those people, you can express why a particular topic means something to you, but it's also important not to waste time forcing an issue if someone isn't interested in exploring.

With limited online resources available about the actual town of Estill and little familial knowledge to go off of, I started doing research on nearby counties in South Carolina, hoping to learn more about the policies, injustices, and paths of my father's people. Through my learnings, I confirmed that following the Civil War, South Carolina took advantage of a loophole in the Thirteenth Amendment that allows for slavery as a punishment for crime and, in turn, widely used the convict lease system to effectively continue enslaving people. Black people were often imprisoned for minor offenses and then leased out for labor, which is something we still see today. And even now, many white South Carolinians choose not to celebrate the Fourth of July but instead observe Confederate Memorial Day to celebrate Confederate values and their reluctance to accept equality and freedom for all. So when I walk around with Southern pride, it's important for me to acknowledge that my pride isn't of the South in totality. Rather, it's rooted in the culture and values my people were able to create despite facing such injustices.

My grandfather Rannell was born in the house that my family in Estill continues to occupy to this day. He met my grandmother Rose at a young age in a nearby town. Estill was so small that everyone knew everyone, and everyone's paths crossed at some point. It was also the kind of town where how you were treated as a Black person was based on your proximity to whiteness—that is, how light or close to white your skin was.

Today the language used within the Black community is still linked to our history in this country and how we've been influenced by white supremacist ideals over time. Growing up, I remember my elders referring to each other as "rednecks" and "whities," but that was just what the darker skin people called the "yellow-boned" members of the family. I never understood these terms to be racist as a child, but I also knew they weren't complimentary. This was often due to the negative reactions they elicited from my lighter-skinned family members. You could always count on someone to laugh or turn beet red while responding with an equally offensive term. To this day, I have an uncle that we refer to as "red daddy." It's laughable to me now, but because he was extremely fair skinned and he would turn bright red in the sun, that's just the name that stuck for him. Our nicknames weren't short references of our names; they were ways in which people could easily differentiate or isolate people based on appearance.

As a child, I also didn't fully grasp the origins of our dialect. I wasn't aware that some of our everyday language was curated with prejudiced undertones. I learned by eavesdropping that skin tone, whether one was "fair-skinned" or "dark-skinned," played a role in how individuals were treated, both within my family and in the outside world. These terms stem from colonialism, which has led to divisions and colorism, not just in America but around the world.

Colorism as a concept is far from new and is often associated with the time when American slavery used a caste-like system that gave lighter-skinned individuals preferential treatment. Lighter-skinned individuals, often of mixed race due to rape by white slave owners, were often subjected to different conditions than their darker-skinned peers and family. This perceived favoritism came with access to the slave master's home and saw them spared from some of the physically strenuous outdoor work. It instead offered domestic indoor jobs, like housekeeping, childrearing, and cooking. Interestingly enough, these very skills set the tone for the roles enslaved people were forced to explore after emancipation. On my father's side, my grandmother and great-aunts all worked as domestic workers for white families.

When my great-aunt Genny was sixteen years old, she moved up north where she would meet her husband, a Black WWII veteran who served with the famed 761st Army Tank Battalion, an independent unit known as the Black Panthers made up mostly of African American soldiers. Her husband ended up dying when I was two years old, and I can't recall ever meeting him, but I always enjoyed spending time with Genny. With so much Black pride, she would tell me stories about her late husband and all they overcame fighting for equality. However, it was strange for me to hear at times because I could never forget family members telling me that Genny was white. Genny's skin was so light that she could pass completely for a white woman, not just someone who was mixed. Despite her outward appearance, she was adamant about identifying solely as Black. She married a browned-skinned Black man and gave birth to a Black son who often wore his hair in a thick Afro. More than anyone, she knew that being partly Black in America didn't garner any special treatment, no matter her genetics or outward proximity to whiteness.

In segregated America, a one-drop rule was established by white men to classify Black people. This rule, frequently applied throughout the twentieth century, insisted that if you had any ounce of Blackness in your DNA, even "one drop," you were considered Black. It was used to further racial segregation and reinforce white supremacy so that even mixed-raced people were denied rights in a white-dominated hierarchy. The implications of this rule were unjust and cruel. One way in which it applied was if a white man fathered a child with a Black woman, the law absolved him of any responsibility. He was not required to provide for the child, and in the cases where the Black woman was enslaved and raped, the child merely represented an increase in property value and labor for the owner. This classification played a major role in how Black people saw themselves back then and even now, and learning about it has helped me understand why Genny saw herself as nothing more than Black. It also helped me understand why it took Black families so long to prioritize unity and raising children in a two-parent household. Black men did not start the phenomenon of father absence.

It's for this reason Black people are so loud about Black pride. It's not to throw our race in the face of others or "make everything about race"; it's simply to change the narrative for ourselves, empower every generation, and help us unlearn what we've historically been told about our hair, speech, appearance, and skills being substandard. This is why we have focused our efforts on campaigns that spark positive thoughts around the word "Black," like the "Black is beautiful" and "Black beauty is beauty" movements.

I believe my father has seen so much throughout his life that he lives with a comparative suffering mindset—when we often feel as though we don't deserve to complain. To this day, he has an admirably optimistic outlook, but I know it stems from our family's deep history of suffering. He always sees his challenging days as "a glass half full," believing that things could always be worse. To know my father is to know he only complains about lazy people, which is also something I've been working to unpack.

Each of us has a story about how our physical appearance once influenced the way others treated us. The quote "don't judge a book by its cover" was in direct response to humans' tendency to observe and create prejudices with very little evidence to go on. But why do we do this? Why do we fixate on our differences? Prejudice is essentially a negative preconception or attitude toward certain groups of people. It significantly affects how individuals behave and interact, especially with those they perceive as different. Often, these prejudiced attitudes are subconscious, influencing someone's behaviors without their awareness.

We've all been influenced to think a certain way or desire a certain lifestyle or look. So when we look to others with judgment, we need to ask ourselves, "Are these thoughts my own?" How much are we influenced by systemic policies, common stereotypes, or our resistance to change? Understanding the historical roots of prejudice is crucial for dismantling discriminatory beliefs and practices in the present. It also highlights the need for active and consistent efforts to rectify historical injustices.

Racial trauma has not only caused self-silencing, but it has caused us to compare ourselves to others based on the treatment we receive.

We need to set ourselves free of this burden so we can grow with change and find comfort in truths. One area of society where we continue to see this issue being perpetuated is in the health-care system and the way it often mistreats and abuses Black patients, who are often viewed as angry or aggressive when what they're often feeling instead is a sense of fear and distrust. This is also why I have family members who are deathly afraid of going to the hospital. It has nothing to do with their injury or health concerns; it's because of how their physical appearance may influence their treatment.

I once read a quote that said, "Prejudice will always be around as long as there is hate." So I think we all need to ask ourselves, What is there to hate about ourselves or others? We cannot judge an entire group of people for the wrongdoings of their ancestors or classify an entire race based on historical or even present actions committed by a very few. Unlearning prejudiced behaviors requires conscious effort, education, and genuine engagement with other groups via conversation, reading their books, and asking about their past.

It's possible you're reading this and have never experienced racial trauma. You may be confident that you're not a racist, and you can't recall a time when you prejudged or mistreated anyone based on their physical appearance. However, the truth is everyone has the capacity to be prejudiced. The difference, though, lies in our level of awareness. Ask yourself the following questions to determine whether or not you carry prejudiced views.

- Are you willing to listen to or converse with someone from a marginalized group as they share their beliefs or perspectives, even if they're different from yours?

- Do you believe every life is equally valuable and important?

- Do your privileges shape the way you treat people who lack those same privileges? For example, have you ever treated someone differently because of their citizenship or lack thereof? An attitude fueled by misconceptions, stereotypes, and xenophobic sentiments portrays migrants as a burden or a threat to society. If you are from a wealthy nation and you look down upon those who are not, that's practicing prejudice.

- Do you make assumptions about people based on their status? For example, have you created assumptions about someone of a particular occupational, educational, financial, or social status?

Our history, despite the pain it holds, offers lessons that can help all of us overcome. Driven by the sacrifices of my ancestors and my parents, I feel a strong sense of responsibility to use my voice in the struggle to dismantle racism in America and hold a mirror to people with prejudiced ideals. It is possible to create a more tolerable and empathetic society if we all step back, take an honest look at ourselves, and consider where the beliefs we hold stem from.

"We must develop and maintain the capacity to forgive. He who is devoid of the power to forgive is devoid of the power to love. There is some good in the worst of us and some evil in the best of us. When we discover this, we are less prone to hate our enemies."

—Martin Luther King Jr.

My father didn't return the rocks that were thrown at him as a child, but he did raise a brave woman who, when confronted with hostility, will stand her ground. Through the lessons shared and the strength I've inherited, I am committed to fighting every day for a more equitable world for my son. I fearlessly challenge people with conversation, and I have no problem holding a mirror up to those who are blind to their biases. In my capacity as the founder of a nonprofit, I lead a diverse team and work with a board that includes many white allies and individuals who value and respect me as a leader. We need more people like them to advance the positive agendas of freedom fighters, stand in solidarity with the Black community, and embrace our cultures while forging lifelong partnerships.

There isn't a day that goes by that I don't think about my race, and it's not because I want to. Oftentimes, this is due to the microaggressions I encounter from some, but mostly it's because of the pride I've built over the years to keep myself encouraged in spaces where I'm not welcomed or appreciated. Each day, I fight and advocate for youth because I recognize their value, and I confront racism and discrimination for the well-being of my father and my family. I want them to see every cycle that I've managed to break and how I've passed on what I've learned. I want people to see a woman who is Black, Latinx, and white who fights for Black liberation because of what her family has come from and because of where she hopes her family will go.

Questions for Yourself

Reflect on the following questions to gauge whether or not there are prejudiced views within your family. After this moment of reflection, consider if your family members would be open to growing beyond their biases and talking about where these thoughts or ideas stem from.

- Are there individuals in your family who are treated unfairly because of their physical appearance or features? Who in the family advocates for them?

- Do you know of any oppressive struggles your family has historically faced? Are there any witnesses or people who may have stories to share about what your family has overcome?

- Were you taught any racist ideologies or ways of thinking by immediate family members?

- Do you know anyone in your family who, due to societal prejudices, was afraid to strive for more because they were taught to be grateful for the minimum?

This moment of introspection is also a good time to use the following questions as a prompt to reflect on the impact of racial discrimination in your own life. If you answer no to the first question, ask a close friend or family member the question, then share how their experience made you feel. The future generations of your family should know about it, so keep a record and pass it on!

- Have you ever been racially profiled or treated differently because of your race or appearance? How did that experience change you?

- When people speak out about the discrimination they or their community has experienced, does it make you feel uncomfortable? If yes, why?

Breaking the Silence of Racial Trauma

Around week twelve of my pregnancy, I found out I was having a male baby. The news brought about a range of emotions, including excitement, relief, and fear. I wondered how I would protect him from those who see him as a threat because he's a Black male. It's bad enough I live in a constant state of concern around my husband's safety as he jogs through our neighborhood where the Black portion of the population is under 3 percent. I worry when he drives because he's often seen as a threatening stereotype and, thus, more likely to get pulled over than I am. I worry because now I will have two Black men to protect.

In today's social climate, people feel more empowered than ever to express their political opinions. People who once hid their prejudiced views in social settings are now loud and proud about what they stand for. Whether that's by waving a particular statement flag outside their home, creating online content to sway the masses, or putting offensive bumper stickers on their car, people are not afraid to discriminate. Some would argue that discourse is getting worse, but I believe that truth provides opportunity for learning, and I would rather know who people really are than have them smile in my face and pretend. Ultimately, I hold onto hope that our truths can bring us together if we learn to listen to each other with empathy and give each other space to express our views in a respectful manner.

> "The only way to undo racism is to consistently identify and describe it—and then dismantle it."
>
> —Ibram X. Kendi

Racial trauma should be openly discussed at home and within your community, but the setting matters. I typically aim to have calm conversations about touchy subjects in small groups or one-on-one situations. When there are important topics being discussed in larger groups, it could unfairly give an advantage to voices in the room that may overpower or dominate the conversation. For a topic that can be so emotionally taxing or triggering, you want to ensure everyone is heard and respected. Exploring the topic of racism doesn't have to feel confrontational. Shift into a mindset that focuses on what your personal objectives are for having the conversation in the first place. Once you've done this, you've made progress. People may not agree with you, but your ideals, once shared, may live rent free in their minds and invite them to think critically about their views.

Initiating conversations about racial discrimination and trauma can evoke discomfort, but it's a topic that can yield positive results if both parties approach the subject with openness. When I respond to racist or prejudiced comments, I also consciously prepare myself to consider that the person I'm addressing may have different levels of bias or awareness when it comes to racial issues. Perhaps they are misinformed, or maybe they don't fully understand the impact racial trauma has on others. Can you be mad at someone for believing a lie? Another thing to remember is that there's misinformation everywhere, and when someone tells you about news or a past experience, remember that you may need to do your own research and explore whether or not it's accurate before you argue or respond.

My hope is that from my ancestors' stories and notable resilience, my son will know his history and take pride in his arrival, knowing that he belongs. I want him to be unapologetically Black in every way, proud like his great-great-aunt Genny and strong like his grandfather—my father, Wallace. I want him to know what his family has overcome and that he stands on the shoulders of indefatigable people who persevered despite facing conditions designed to break them. Armed with ancestral knowledge, he will understand the pressure that comes with being from a lineage of men who were not seen as equal. From my family on both sides, my son will see his potential to continue healing for those who didn't know how. What will the generations that come after you learn from your family's resilience?

Healer's Recap

- What defense mechanisms have you created to protect yourself from your emotional wounds?

- Be direct in your questioning to family members; it may be the only way to get your answers.

- Racism cannot and should not be denied. It is physically and mentally harmful for all who experience it, regardless of age, gender, or economic status.

- Comparative suffering is something we can all relate to, and when we do, we often feel as though we don't deserve to complain. We do. Our pain is valid and worth expressing.

- Take pride in your culture, your people, and your community.

- "Prejudice will always be around as long as there is hate."

- People may not agree with you, but your ideals, once shared, may live rent free in their minds and invite them to think critically about their beliefs.

Chapter Six

Who Is God to You?

Do you own your faith?

My father never came to church with us, but I didn't know the reason until I was much older and finally asked my mother why. "Your father doesn't believe in God anymore," she gently explained. "When your father's first cousin and best friend passed away, he stayed up at the hospital praying all night. He asked God to save him, and unfortunately He didn't. When your cousin passed, your father was so heartbroken that he lost his faith." I empathized with my father and didn't pry for more information. I imagined myself in that situation, praying on my knees in the hospital, leaning completely on my faith for a miracle. If I were in that situation, with limited understanding of God's favor or how any of this works, I would've been hurt too.

Recently, I asked my father if he had memories of any religious expressions his mother used when he was growing up. One that stood out to him the most was, "God will make it right; don't worry." There it was! Instantly I could see why he grew up believing that God would fix all things and spare life. By asking this simple question, I was able to put some of the pieces together and understand his unrealistic expectations of God.

Pain is inevitable, but that doesn't make it fair. When terrible things happen to us, regardless of how deep our faith may be, we often ask, "Why me? Of the eight billion people in the world, why was I chosen for this path?" It's a question that we can never get a solid answer to, but we can draw from our strength and push through to overcome and find meaning in our pain.

People find and lose their faith every day for a multitude of reasons, perhaps due to their personal beliefs about how God should operate or how life should progress. Regardless, this is a deeply personal choice influenced by their religion and experiences. My father had a specific request for God. When his prayers weren't answered, he let his disappointment diminish his faith. He didn't consider that pain is not a punishment or that there may have been reasons for his loss that weren't meant to be explained right away. It's a tough mindset to grapple with, but one that I've found brings peace in dark times.

> "Trust in the Lord with all your heart and lean not
> on your own understanding; in all your ways submit
> to Him, and He will make your paths straight."
>
> —Proverbs 3:5–6 (NKJV)

Our expectations of favor, our desire for immediate answers, and our need for confirmation that our prayers are being heard can either draw us closer to our faith or lead us to abandon our religious beliefs altogether. Is your relationship with God conditional?

I didn't grow up with a manual of how to build a healthy relationship with God. I was left to figure it out on my own. When I was in elementary school, my grandmother Rose gave me a black leather Bible with my name engraved on it. It was by far the most voluminous and challenging read I had received up until that point, but I looked forward to diving in. After all, I had plenty of time on my hands, and it was a nice change from my Babysitters Club and Goosebumps chapter reads. My goal was to read the Bible from front to back. It was an ambitious goal, but I was up for the challenge. Word after word, I attempted to make sense of the unfamiliar terms and would dissect the parts that sounded similar to my typical reads. It was my first time engaging with the Bible outside of hearing a pastor recite specific passages, and I had no idea what I was doing, but I sure did try to figure it out.

At times, I would start reading and get distracted, repeatedly picking up the Bible and putting it down after a few pages. Each time, I'd forget what I had read, forcing me to restart more times than I can count. Looking back now, I think I somehow believed I was reading a full story that could only be understood in the order it was written. The Bible didn't come with instructions, and I wasn't about to go to my dad and ask if he knew what I should be doing. So I created this idea in my mind that I had to read the entire Bible and that this was an obligation all humans were supposed to take at some point in their lives. I wanted to know God's story and why church was so important.

Back when I lived in the Bronx, my mother would dress me and my brother up on Easter Sunday and take us to church. However, when we moved to Long Island and my parents separated, my great-aunt Genny and my grandmother Rose would take me to church instead. My dad and my brother always stayed back, but I didn't mind. Genny and Rose were devoted Christians, never missing a Sunday, and they were grooming me in a sense to carry on their traditions.

Church felt like a joyous space, a place where people came together to feel and leave well, and I appreciated that. On Sundays, it wasn't hard for me to choose between going into that space or staying home in my room with my thoughts. Church was a place that made me feel energized, from the soul claps to the singing to the passionate preaching and smiling strangers. Even when the message went completely over my head and even in the heat, working my arm with the paper fan, I felt good. I felt like I was doing something good with my time by worshiping—at least that's what my elders taught me.

Sunday service was long, but I looked forward to the choir, and I always found the pastor to be quite animated and entertaining. Everything about the Baptist church experience differed from how I saw people show up throughout the week. At church, we "put on our Sunday's best," and the men, women, and children would show up and show out. Then there was me, with my one dress that I would recycle each week with my kitten heels. That was the best I could do. Tucked right beside my elders, I would sit cross-legged and quiet just as the other children were taught to do.

The Black church has provided hope and comfort to my family for generations. The history of the Black church can be traced back to a time when Sunday morning was the only time enslaved people could momentarily step away from the fabric scraps and harsh realities of their lives to express themselves through faith and fashion. In fact, in order for slave owners to be considered "good," they had to permit their slaves to attend church and provide them with at least one church outfit. Black enslaved women who could sew would add their own touches to the clothing, finding ways to express themselves or stand out with their families. It was the only time enslaved people were free to be social and gather with others. As time went on, this practice of putting on your Sunday's best would allow for newly free people, often with limited means, to invest in their finest suits, dresses, and church crowns—also known as church hats. These head coverings, referenced in the Bible, became more elaborate with time, with Black women adding sequins, ribbons, feathers, and more to stand out among their fellow worshippers and make a statement. In this way, church fashion was a form of resistance. It was about more than just dressing to worship. For Black people in America, it was a testament to their unbreakable spirit, and it gave them more reason to craft moments of pride and celebration in their limited communal space. It was their moment to be noticed.

My grandmother Rose exemplified this tradition. She opted for casual and budget-friendly fashion from Monday to Saturday, always carrying the same black shoulder bag that held a day's worth of mints and a white washcloth to collect the sweat from the hot sun. On Sundays, however, she would go into her closet and pull out one of her best dresses (the ones wrapped in plastic) and her kitten heels (a big change from her everyday skippies), and she'd strategically choose from her collection of church hats to cover her crown. She would transform for Sunday service, and she seemed to love doing so. Church was my grandmother's escape. In many ways, I think she believed she could pray away her grief and daily stressors. She held tight to this hope that God would make everything right in her world, and for two hours when she was there, He did. The Black church was her therapy.

For centuries, people attended church for emotional and communal support. It was a destination for healing when professional therapeutic advice wasn't accessible, especially for minorities. In a recent Pew Research Center study, 88 percent of African Americans affirmed their belief in God with absolute certainty.[1] This study suggests that Black people generally exhibit a strong connection to religious beliefs, which could be due to many of us growing up in the Christian church and being told that the journey to salvation would take place only when we give our lives, our troubles, and our worries to the Lord.

When you walk into a church, you will find people hoping to cover their inadequacies with prayer or wash away their transgressions with forgiveness when, really, they also may need therapy, the pastor included. But you can't tell my grandmother this. She will die with her pastor on a pedestal. She believed that he lived as an example of how God wanted us to live our lives. If you asked me, I would tell you she didn't know that man at all. If we grew up accustomed to showing up as our representatives on Sundays, wearing things we wouldn't typically wear Monday through Friday, what made my grandmother believe that everyone was showing up to church as their authentic selves?

In my line of work, connecting and building genuine friendships with pastors across the US, I've come to understand that pastors are people who need help and prayer just like the rest of us. Our strongest leaders often face the biggest challenges, and even after finding God, some can still struggle silently alongside their congregants with addiction, unhealed trauma, and unhealthy familial and romantic relationships. These same pastors conceal their brokenness once they approach the altar. They often fear that revealing their vulnerabilities would result in losing support and followers, and they're not wrong to feel this way. Historically, this is one of the biggest issues within the church, spreading the idea that we need to portray an image of spiritual perfection and strength in order to be listened to and taken seriously. Yet I wonder, What does it truly mean to commit ourselves to Christ if authenticity and honesty are absent beyond the confines of the sanctuary?

The elders in my family were intentional about preserving the tradition of living God-like and attending church. My grandmother was always the first to point out a sinner. Very serious about her religious practices, she even stopped drinking one day after making a promise to God that she would never drink again because of an early morning hangover. She was faithful to the end and wanted her family so badly to follow her ways. She would turn her nose up and shake her head at the shenanigans at family BBQs and tell all of us that we needed Jesus.

My grandmother hoped that, through me, she could redevelop the cycle of faithfulness and prayer that my parents seemingly fell out of. My brother had no interest in going, but I wasn't so hard to convince. I was longing for something I couldn't explain at the time, and the church seemed to pour into me in ways I needed. I still experience that feeling I felt as a child when I'm in church today, but I don't show up the same. I go to church to hear the word, tithe to support the local programs my church offers the community, and feel soul-full.

I know my sense of spiritual kinship is not a universal experience. For some, the messages preached don't resonate, leaving them feeling alienated or unworthy of belonging, particularly when a preacher's words cast seeds of doubt about their righteousness. People have always used religion as a weapon to control others. Even during slavery, as free as African Americans wished to be, if whites were in attendance, the white or slave preachers would encourage obedience to slave masters. Surveys from the 1800s revealed testimonials that revealed how religion was experienced by enslaved Black peoples. "Before freedom we always went to white churches on Sundays with passes, but they never mentioned God; they always told us to be 'good niggers and mind our missus and masters,'" said Clayborn Gantling, enslaved in Georgia.[2]

Another testimony reads, "De slaves went to church wid dey marsters. De preachers always preached to de white folks first, den dey would preach to de slaves. Dey never said nothin' but you must be good, don't steal, don't talk back at your masters, don't run away, don't do dis, and don't do dat," Leah Garett recalled, enslaved in Georgia.[3]

"I have heard it said that Tom Ashbie's father went to one of the cabins late at night, the slaves were having a secret prayer meeting. He heard one slave ask God to change the heart of his master and deliver him from slavery so that he may enjoy freedom. Before the next day the man disappeared, no one ever seeing him again . . . When old man Ashbie died, just before he died, he told the white Baptist minister that he had killed Zeek for praying and that he was going to hell," Silas Jackson said, enslaved in Virginia.[4]

These testimonials showcase how difficult and long the journey has been for African Americans to find God apart from any controlled narratives. They also helped me understand just how complicated many of our relationships with God still are today. Sometimes our view of God or a higher power has more to do with who introduced us and our childhood experiences. There was a time when one community church or one preacher's word meant absolute truth to their congregation. Now, we are privileged to understand that a pastor's message is simply their interpretation of the Bible, and we can either agree or disagree with that. We also have the option to "shop around" for spiritual guidance, much like we would search for the right therapist. With the diverse perspectives and intentions people bring to religion, we have the power to choose which Bible interpretations we follow. Following every voice is not our purpose, and some spiritual homes are not meant to be our house of worship.

For generations, people have twisted the words of the Bible to promote negative ideologies with interpretations far beyond the original meaning. And for centuries, preachers have weaponized the Bible to serve their own agendas, turning its text into a tool that promotes exclusion and intolerance, which have turned many community members away from their pews. This manipulation is a testament to the power of interpretation, highlighting how the same text can be used to both unite and divide, depending on the interpreter's intent. The little girl in me who had no guidance and didn't know how to understand the Bible would've fallen for anything. It took years of trying different churches, finding God within, and engaging deeply in Bible study to fully grasp where I stand on religion.

I do not blame or judge those who have distanced themselves from the church or turned away from religious upbringings to embrace atheism. However, I often find myself wanting to ask them if they see aspects of God in any parts of their life or in the people around them. Does this in any way give them hope? I wonder if it's the beliefs or generational outdated religious practices of others that have pushed them away. Folks often react strongly to manipulation, emotional dependency, and exploitation, as people leverage their position of authority and economic control. And unfortunately, the Word has been manipulated for years, and the church has held more power over the community and its most vulnerable members. But there's a major shift that's taking place with the younger generations that are now questioning everything, placing the power back into the community, and reshaping the way they choose to practice.

How much do you know about your ancestors' relationship with God? Do you think they would respect the shifts you've made in your spiritual journey? In forming our opinions about religion, we must consider that it operates differently for everyone; there is no right or wrong way to believe unless those beliefs harm individuals or groups of people.

Most faiths have unique sacred texts; for instance, Muslims have the Quran, Hindus have the Vedas, and Buddhists have their sutras. The compilation of stories sacred to Christians is referred to as the Bible. These stories were compiled over centuries, with the earliest books written around 1200 BC and the latest by approximately 100 AD, in a time when traditional values and human rights were drastically different. So when we cite sacred texts today without considering these changes, it can lead to interpretations that do not align with modern views and practices of equality and justice. For instance, preachers have frequently referenced Leviticus 18:22 (NIV) as evidence of the Bible's stance against same-sex relationships: "Do not have sexual relations with a man as one does with a woman; that is detestable." But there are practitioners who do not agree with this interpretation.

A recent Pew Research Center survey of over 8,600 Black American adults found that young Black adults are less religious and less engaged in Black churches than older generations.[5] In speaking with Reverend Toni Ingram of the famous African Methodist Episcopal Church in Georgia, I learned that she holds a master's degree in Intentional Intergenerational Ministry. She dedicated part of her career to reconnecting with younger generations, whom she believed felt marginalized or overlooked by church communities and their elders. She shared, "The issue for the Black church has been that even though it's supposedly a place of liberation and freedom and encouragement, it has also become a place of patriarchy, homophobic mistreatments, [and] sexism, and people can't find their way. At some point we stopped being concerned about the rights of all folks and started subscribing to what would be right in the lives of a particular few, so that we could culturally be in line with what other people were doing. You have to participate and look and dress in ways that are socially acceptable."

We all know somebody who acts holy one day a week. We also know people who project their fears on others by belittling or rejecting what they perceive to be different. They are oftentimes the same individuals who would insist on promoting outdated interpretations of the Bible or pass down such prejudicial ideas to younger generations. I can't help but wonder why they seek to preserve tradition at the expense of progress and inclusivity. What is the deeper reluctance to embrace the evolution of change? If it's not harming anyone, what's so scary about allowing others to choose how they wish to live?

In Mark 9:24, a father brings his son, who had been possessed by a spirit that caused him to have convulsions, to the disciples for healing. After they tried unsuccessfully to heal the boy, the father turned to Jesus as his last hope. When Jesus encountered the father and his son, He spoke about the power of faith. In response to Jesus's comment that "everything is possible for one who believes," the father exclaimed, "I believe; help my unbelief!" This poignant expression captures the father's complex emotional state. He has faith in Jesus's power to heal his son, yet he also recognizes his doubts and the limitations of his faith.

I often think about the people, namely the children we work with, who suffer from life's toughest challenges and how they're able to hold on to their faith. In an effort to find some answers, I reached out to author and reverend Dr. Darrell Armstrong, a man of deep faith who was adopted as a child. I remembered hearing his testimony, and I wanted to know more about how he found God along his journey—a journey in which religion was not introduced by his biological parents. He shared:

"My best advice to those who are seeking to 'better understand' God is to start with the concept that God is personal and desires an individual relationship. As a pastor, I often cite phrases such as: 'God is more interested in *relationship* than in *membership*!' or 'There is a difference between *religion* and *spirituality*,' or simply 'Don't put God in a box!' These phrases suggest the notion that there are two lenses through which to see God: (1) a terrestrial, bottom-up, divine lens and (2) the celestial, top-down, divine lens. The former is shaped by routine, ritual, doctrine, and dogma—all of which are defined by limitations and localities. The latter is shaped by freedom, openness, fullness, and those things which are defined by destinations and possibilities."

In response to me asking where his faith journey began, he responded, "As a child, I had what some Christian denominationalists call M-A-C-E Christianity: [when you only attend service on] Mother's Day, Advent, Christmas, and Easter. However, when my brother and I were removed from our mother's custody due to repeated child abuse and poverty-related issues of neglect, my faith journey took on a new dimension. Through several foster home placements, with families who were strangers, I had to depend on God in a new and different way. However, it was my long-term placement with my maternal grandfather and my step-grandmother that transformed my understanding of and dependence upon God."

Reverend Armstrong continued, "My grandfather was not a particularly religious man; his southern roots in Arkansas cultivated a deep respect for the church. He strongly endorsed his wife, my step-grandmother, to take her five biological children and me, her new step-grandson, to church. Thus began my true religious journey, at the age of eight, of regularly attending church and being captivated by my Sunday school teachers and mesmerized by my then pastor, the late Rev. Dr. Richmond Brown."

I found it interesting that Reverend Armstrong's grandfather was not religious yet wanted his grandchildren to know God and attend service. I believe that sometimes we want things for ourselves but aren't willing to do the work, so we desire for our children to have them instead. It's easier to say the next generation will do it.

Who Introduced You to God?

I know my grandmother, my great-aunt, and at some point all of my family believed in God, but I don't know to what extent they relinquished power and control to God. What I do know is that they gave Him their grief, dreams, and worries and lived in His example in hopes of eternal life. The demonstration of their faith was heard in the songs they played at home, in their church attendance, and in all of the praying they did to make sure the family was well.

If you ask people "Who is God to you?" you will get a different answer every time. For me, God started as an idea, a spiritual presence that was everywhere and watching over everything. When I was alone in my bed at night, I spoke to Him. And before I went to sleep, I wrote to Him in my faith journal, a place where every page began with "Dear God." I often preferred to write instead of getting on my knees. In my conversations with God, I would ask a lot of whys and try to make sense of my family's separation. Then I would do the traditional stuff: I would thank Him for my family before dinners and ask Him to keep me safe when traveling. I was somewhat in a routine with our connection and didn't necessarily know if that was normal or not. As a child, aside from writing God letters, I mimicked what my mother and the elders did.

My religious practices were good for me. Having God to turn to helped keep me sane during some of my darkest days, and going to church gave me the hope and empowerment I needed to feel energized. But unlike my elders, I'm not worried about what anyone else is doing, and I'm not looking to any people or church staff to demonstrate how I should or shouldn't live my life. I'm content with how I show up in the world Monday through Sunday, even when I need to watch church from home instead of attending in person.

When I was in the fourth grade, I fell in love with the Joan Osbourne song "One of Us." Her lyrics felt so real to me. It wasn't a praise record; it was a song about seeing God in us, in the ordinary, and in the people we hold lowest in society. It addressed issues that come up in the Bible like inequality, societal hierarchies, and suffering. I felt as though Joan was singing for herself, hoping to see God in her similar struggles or for the world to reimagine the way they see and connect with Him. I think she hoped others would see Him not as some higher power that looks down on us but a spark of divinity that lives in us and connects us to one another, no person being higher or better than the other. I'd often listen to that song on repeat, and apparently so did the rest of the world. It went on to win a Grammy for Song of the Year and Record of the Year in 1996.

The song helped people reconsider what we've been taught: that God above looks down on the world. But it's possible that God is not simply a being in a high place that looks down on us; rather, He is the love around us, the comfort it lends, and the people who inspire us to be the greatest version of ourselves. In that song, just as in the hymns I overheard Grandma Rose sing daily, I felt a yearning for hope and leaned into that curiosity. I started thinking about the human experience a bit differently, wondering who we all really are and if any of us are traveling spirits. As a child, I was excited to hear from someone who imagined what the presence of God could feel like in everyday situations. It was a foreign concept to me and probably the start of my true spiritual journey. It was the start of a faith that has no guilty conscience if I miss a Sunday service because I'm content with my attempts of praise and worship throughout the week. I'm content believing that God sees me still, and He's in the person that I touch and love each day.

My faith has evolved and will likely continue to over time. Throughout adulthood, my relationship has shifted from wondering what God was to feeling His presence inside of me. Thinking of God can turn my whole day around, and leaning on Him makes me feel like everything is okay, even when it's not. This is the belief that was passed down, but it took a different approach for me to trust in my relationship with God.

Many people in the Black community used church for mental health support before therapy was an option, and churches were the first stop for community members in need of social services. It was and still is where people go to understand their trauma. I believe the church kept my grandmother well in the mind, at least well enough to stop herself from falling apart when the pain felt impossible to endure. I could see that for her because I remember times when I felt broken or hopeless, and a Sunday service was able to restore my faith. Interestingly, my father has regained his faith in God. He even speaks freely about God now and shares prayers via text, which is something I didn't witness in my younger years. I'm not sure what pivotal moment sparked the change for him, but I'm grateful. I'm grateful to see him grow.

Questions for Yourself

This is the only part of the book where I will encourage you to get silent. Because I believe religion and spirituality are intertwined, I feel that sometimes we need to quiet the noise of the chants around us, the choir in front of us, or the family traditions we've acquired to tap into our spiritual needs or religious beliefs. Sometimes we just need silence to hear what's true for us. To facilitate a space of silence and reflection, start by asking yourself the following questions:

- What religious cycles have I broken? When reflecting on this question, consider whether or not you're content with breaking those cycles or if you would like to redevelop some of your previous traditions.

- What cycles will I continue? This doesn't have to be something you've done up until this point. This question can be used as a revelation on what cycle you would like to build back or strengthen.

- What is prayer to me? Do I recite set prayers, meditate, or recite mantras? Do I speak out loud or use my internal voice? Prayer should feel like an extremely personal experience. It is your own internal dialogue, spiritual connection, or communication line to the divine. I encourage you to recognize when and how you're praying and decide if that's working for you.

God and religion are topics I'm comfortable talking about, and knowing that we all hold unique relationships with Him, I often ask my friends where they are on their spiritual journeys. Although these are very personal questions, I've found that being open to each other's varying beliefs has only brought us closer, and it's good practice for conversations with family members. I asked two of my closest friends the questions I just posed to you in the previous section. What follows are their responses.

I'm lucky to call Grammy Award–winning singer and songwriter Miguel one of my best friends, and we speak about religion and spirituality often. Miguel grew up with a mother who was a Jehovah's Witness, and understandably she had very serious expectations that her children practice the religion as well. Jehovah's Witnesses emphasize the use of Jehovah as God's name and are well-known for their door-to-door evangelism, traveling by foot to spread their interpretation of the Bible and invite others to join in their faith. Unique to their religion, they also stay neutral on political matters and refrain from celebrating traditional Christian holidays and birthdays.

Miguel has come a long way in figuring out what religious practices matter most to him. Here are his responses to my questions:

> My beliefs have changed from the traditional Christian model I was taught as a child. I still go to God as a father figure and at the same time I imagine Him as a universal energy I'm always connected to. I also believe God is less dogmatic than I was raised to believe Him to be. For future generations, I want to teach by example that God is within and it's important to be deeply connected to God on an inner personal level, and if so, He will shine through in your choices.
>
> Prayer to me is like a first act of faith that a greater all-powerful love exists. I've come to realize that I don't meditate when I'm looking for guidance; I pray to Jehovah and finish through Jesus Christ. When I want to manifest something, I meditate. And when I'm feeling gratitude and overwhelmed with joy, I thank God and the universe.

In the same group chat, I turned the question on my other best friend Ro James, who is a Grammy-nominated singer. Ro grew up in the church, and his father was a pastor, preacher, and military drill sergeant. Here's what he shared:

> God is in everything and is everything. When I was a kid I used to think God was in the sky looking down on me with Jesus and the Holy Ghost watching everything I did from heaven, judging me. I was taught that every mistake made was a mark against me getting into heaven. As I got older, while seeking understanding and purpose, I learned to develop my own personal relationship with God. Now I believe that God is me and I am God. Through my understanding of how God forgives, I've

learned to be more forgiving than the generations prior to me. Not that I have mastered it, but I understand.

I hope to teach my daughter to love like "Christ" and I want to pass on my newer learnings that God is also energy, vibration, the sun, the moon, and everything in between. That's something that's not taught at church. Back in the day, this way of thinking was said to be witchcraft, when in reality it leans into intuition and discernment. I challenge everything in the Bible, and my daughter will as well. I want her to seek the truth rather than believe what's told as the absolute truth.

Something that really stood out to me in Ro's response was his understanding that mistakes will impact his final journey. That made me think about how many people often pray for forgiveness for their sins, and I wondered if we focus on forgiving ourselves in the process. Ro's response was an interesting reminder that we often teach our children that they should anticipate being judged, not just by others but by a higher power. We pass on the fear that imperfection requires forgiveness, and without it, our destiny is questioned.

After reflecting on my spiritual and religious journeys, I decided to write a letter to my grandmother Rose. Rose is still alive today, but she has dementia and is unable to read. The last time I saw her was about four years ago during a hospital stay. As I was saying my good-byes, she looked at me with a smile and said, "Yes, mom." The fact that my grandmother didn't recognize me as "Coley" didn't seem to bother me. At that moment, I realized she saw me as something she needed. Living most of her life without her mother's presence, leaving the South at a young age, and losing her husband after creating an entirely new world and family with him, her journey has been long. God was her guide and hope through it all, but in the end perhaps what she really needed during those difficult times was her mom. Even though my grandmother can't read my letter, it doesn't mean I can't read it to her or express my feelings to her.

Dear Grandma,

I wish we could talk and you could tell me stories about how you were introduced to the church. I'm so curious about how you found your faith and whether or not you always believed. I want you to know that I too love gospel music, and I've found a couple church homes that suit my needs. I also have friends that are leadership members of the church, and I work closely with pastors all across the country to organize volunteer initiatives to support the cities' most hungry and vulnerable youth. Each time I step on a church stage, I think about your Sunday attire, stockings and shoes. I think about your love for God and how you passed that on to me.

I know you are not perfect, but none of us are. What I've come to believe about religion is that it's not about pretending to have it all together but being honest about our shortcomings and vulnerabilities that bring us closer to salvation. God loves all of His children just as they are.

Dad believes in God again. One day, out of nowhere, he just started saying things like "God bless you" and "I'm praying for this person or that person." I think everyone around him was so happy to see the change that none of us actually asked what happened to help him redevelop his faith—but does it even matter?

Because of you, I will continue to praise God and pass the Word down to my child. I will teach him what I know but let him decide what works best for him. Your Bible will live in this family for centuries to come.

I'm praying for you, Grandma.

—Nicole

The Bible my grandma Rose gave me sits in my home to this day. I treasure it as the greatest gift I've ever received, and one day I will add my child's name to it and pass it on, not for its messaging, but because of what it represents for our family and history. I want to be loud about my faith, especially now that I've come to own it.

Healer's Recap

- There is no one way to experience God.

- Do not place judgment upon anyone for their religious preferences. People find and lose their faith every day for a multitude of reasons.

- Be cautious of people who use religion as a weapon to control others.

- Church is not a replacement for therapy. They can work hand in hand.

- Consider what religious cycles you wish to pass on or break for future generations.

- Remember that prayer is personal. Never apologize for your differences.

Chapter Seven

Violence Epidemic

Healing begins by telling the truth.

—Dr. Joy Degruy

Are you connected to anyone who displays aggressive behavior toward themselves or others?

I carry secrets I will take to the grave to protect those who aren't ready to share their truths. My role in their stories isn't that of a witness but rather a confidant. I believe it is not my place to disclose the traumas they endured. However, for those who have confided in me about their traumatic experiences, I offer my prayers for their healing, I encourage them to seek justice, and I assure them of my support whenever they need someone to talk to. Whether they're dealing with past experiences related to racial trauma, domestic violence, sexual assault, suicidal attempts, abuse, or murder, far too many people walk with shame, afraid of facing the truth and choosing to deliberately ignore the past.

Violence, whether endured or inflicted, touches all of our ancestors, yet it remains one of the most avoided topics within the home. Deciding whether a secret, especially one regarding violence or abuse, should be held in or set free can leave someone feeling conflicted for their entire life. On one end you want to be loyal, but safeguarding the truth often demands careful consideration because in many cases it means no justice.

Violence has many masks. Growing up in New York City, it's something that I not only experienced but commonly observed. As a result, even something as innocent as a midday stroll requires me to be mentally prepared to react fast or dodge danger. Many people live in this type of fear every day, approaching new environments and experiences with this level of caution, coupled with inescapable thoughts about potential violence. This hypervigilance mindset can stem from past traumas, and for some, it's an unshakable fear. It's a mentality birthed from anxiety that insists danger lurks around every corner and anyone could be plotting harm at any moment. It can impact where someone will ultimately choose to live and work, how they'll spend their leisure time, and which safety or defensive behaviors they'll act out day to day.

Living in a hypervigilance mindset and displaying safety behaviors like freeze, flee, resist, defend, control, or fight are common for people who have experienced significant trauma. Any possible threat can activate these anxiety-driven protective behaviors, and they don't even have to be anything directly life-threatening. Anything that has the potential to cause pain and suffering, like financial or food insecurity, verbal or emotional aggression, or even the transmission of an illness, is enough to keep us in a state of hypervigilance. These experiences contribute to an atmosphere of mistrust, where every unknown face might hide an assailant, and every interaction must be approached with hesitancy and caution. The sheer thought of a potentially dangerous situation compels individuals suffering from hypervigilance to guard themselves against unfavorable possibilities. The body's response to these occurrences can manifest both physically and psychologically, influencing one's ability to show up authentically each day.

Our negative experiences, even those in our dreams, impact how we move today. One time I was walking in Times Square and a complete stranger stabbed me in the leg. It was an unprovoked attack by someone I imagine suffered from mental illness. He stabbed me so fast that by the time I processed what happened and why there was a large slice in my jeans, he was able to get away. Another time in Brooklyn, a complete stranger walked up to me on a crowded A train and began to curse me out. He was completely unaware of who I was, but in his mind I was someone from his past. Although I tried to tell him I didn't know him, he spit on me and then approached me with his fists clutched tight, inches away from my face. Thankfully a brave stranger jumped in to fight for me, but ever since then I've tried my best to avoid taking the A train.

Some of the cautious thoughts I carry are inherited fears and nightmares that were passed down to me by my father. He was not only a protector of his children and family, but he was always ready for war. This may be partly why I live in a constant state of hypervigilance. Over the years, I've essentially tricked my mind into believing that my strategic movements are the reason for my safety, and this mindset in particular has allowed this practice to become a habit. I remember being this way even as far back as elementary school, hearing the loudspeaker announcements about suspicious white vans and strangers who followed children home from school. These announcements would leave me and the rest of the students afraid and left to converse with each other about what was happening and how to keep ourselves safe. Rumors would swirl, and students would talk about scary stories of people they knew who were almost taken. This fear that was placed in me by adults caused a level of anxiety that I was completely unaware of at the time. It caused me to fixate on the possibilities of getting kidnapped every single day as I walked home from the school bus. So naturally, I had to make sure this wasn't going to be my fate. This hyperfixation on preventing my kidnapping led me to have repetitive nightmares about that very scenario.

As a young child, I had frequent nightmares. Oftentimes I knew I was dreaming, and I would wake up in a pool of sweat, afraid of what would've happened if I hadn't jolted myself awake just before matters got worse. Back then, regardless of how hard I tried to think of positive things at bedtime, I continued to experience similar dreams, and with each one, I woke up more curious about what would happen if I fought back or escaped. If I stayed in the dream until the end, perhaps it would lessen my fear and help prepare me for this possible reality. So I chose to fight back.

Each night I found new, creative ways to escape my captors, and I started to gain confidence in my ability to navigate every type of kidnapping known to man. At the time I had no idea I was "lucid dreaming," or dreaming in a state of semi-awareness. Looking back, I realize I was often using "reality testing," a technique that helped me decide if I was having a lucid dream. How did I know how to do this? I have no idea, but the theory is if you do reality testing regularly, these habits will also form in your dreams.

Reality testing is exactly what it sounds like: testing out different hypotheses to determine whether or not a dream is real. Engaging in this process each night eventually helped me confront my fears of kidnapping, practice self-defense skills, and activate my problem-solving capabilities. By questioning my dreams as well as reality, I was also able to develop a deeper understanding of my subconscious mind. When I knew for sure that what I was experiencing in my dream wasn't real, I'd often ask myself, *What are my dreams trying to tell me?* and *What can I learn from this situation?*

This ability to tap in and recognize when you're dreaming isn't easy, but mastering control over the dream realm through lucid dreaming helped instill a strong sense of agency and strength in me as a child. It provided me with a sense of control during a time when I almost let fear take over both my dreaming and waking life. For anyone who's interested in lucid dreaming to quell nightmares or simply get curious about the dream state, I encourage you to try the following techniques in your dream:

- **MIRRORS**: Try to find your reflection in a dream. When dreaming, reflections may appear distorted or unusual, which can help you recognize you're in a dream state.

- **HANDS**: Look down at your hands. If dreaming, your hands will likely appear deformed and/or if you try to count your fingers, the number will be off or continue to change.

- **PHONES AND COMPUTERS:** Turn on your phone or computer to see if the background is correct and if the apps are as you remember. This is often something that dreams fail to get right.

- **TIME:** Look for a watch or clock. Monitoring time through clocks can help you determine if you're having real-time experiences. In dreams, time tends to fluctuate erratically.

- **BREATHING:** Hold your breath by tightly sealing your nose. If you can still breathe, you're dreaming.

One day my dreams caught up to me. After years of navigating nightmares of being kidnapped in my childhood, someone attacked me on the very street I imagined in my dreams, turning my fears into reality. I was in my early twenties when the incident occurred, coming home late from working at a lounge in NYC. At that time, I was living back home with my father in hopes of saving money, and as much as I dreaded taking the Long Island Rail Road so late, I feared the walk from the train station back to my home even more. At night, Long Island was a quiet place with little audio stimulation aside from the crickets. So every night, and with every walk, I kept my senses on high alert.

That night, fear set in as I noticed a strange man hiding behind a fence along my path. I couldn't see his entire body, but his face was clearly visible. In a moment of panic, I anxiously searched for my phone and called my mom to tell her what was going on. Despite living so far away, I knew she would pick up no matter the hour. With each cautious step closer to where he hid, I quietly talked to my mom, hoping to avoid drawing more of his attention. Mustering the courage to cross the street, I put some distance between us so I could pass him without getting too close. Now with the stranger behind me, I remembered thinking to myself, *If this asshole messes with me, I'm going to kill him.* That was the result of the courage I had worked up over my many years of reality testing in my sleep. The pep talk worked.

I only had two more blocks before I made it home, but those two blocks felt like ten. Suddenly as I was approaching the corner of my street, I heard his footsteps pounding the pavement. He was running toward me full speed. Not clearly thinking—or maybe I was—I decided to turn around and wait for him to approach me. Yup, I positioned myself, ready to fight as if I prepared for this moment. Ignoring my mother's screams on the other end of the phone, I put up my hands and I started screaming, "I'm going to fucking kill you. You better not fucking touch me. I'm crazy!" Had I ever talked to any man like this before? Yes, in my dreams!

The man reached to grab me and my flailing arms, and I blocked every attempt. He continuously shouted, "Be quiet. Shut up. Shut up," but I only got louder. I could sense my fear had been transferred to him. The man, puzzled and confused, decided the fight wasn't worth it and ran off, leaving me standing there in complete shock.

My father doesn't fear people, but I believe he fears the inability to protect, a fear of not being prepared for the worst-case scenario. He exhibits safety behaviors at all times, ready to take out whoever becomes a threat to him or his family, and this is often a needed defense mechanism. But when it's chronic and unnecessary, it can pose many problems, not just to him but to his descendants too. My inherited need to stay on high alert is not just our personal burden; it's a historical echo, a reminder of the struggles and dangers our ancestors faced. It's a result of our mothers teaching us to remain alert, conscious of the fact that, to some, we were born a threat, perceived as violent or problematic because of our skin color. It's our strategy for survival, a cycle that I'm afraid I'll need to repeat.

Back in high school I remember my father heard a commotion outside while he was cleaning the kitchen. He looked and found two robbers hopping our fence to get away after breaking into a neighbor's home. Instantly, without thought, my father ran out back to stop them. He didn't consider that the guys could've been armed and dangerous or that they could have caused him bodily injury. Instead, he leaped into action to protect his community. My father, with his bare hands and a shovel he picked up along his run through the backyard, caught the two men and held them down for about fifteen seconds before the cops arrived. Apparently they had already been chasing the guys, yet when they arrived, they treated my father like a criminal. With guns drawn, they yelled for him to drop his "weapon," the shovel.

At the time I remembered feeling so concerned about the risks associated with my father's actions. He compromised his own safety to help a neighbor, and then the cops put his life at risk for being in the wrong place (on his property) at the wrong time with a garden tool. Considering the harsh realities of police brutality against Black people, I thought about how wrong things could have gone. I could've lost my father in a moment's notice. I had seen him stick up for family members in the past but never for complete strangers. Who did he think he was?

My father isn't afraid of violence. I don't think any of the Russells are. We're truly a special bunch. My father didn't run from danger; he prepared for it. A natural protector, he was always lifting weights or fight training. My father is strong and brave, and he wanted everyone in the community to know that our house was not a stop you ever wanted to make if you're up to trouble. He told my brother and I that he would do anything for us and go to jail if he had to. He never wanted us to question if he had our backs or if he was capable of protecting us. I never really wondered why he said it so often, but I believed him so much that I grew to become an adult who craved protection and security within my romantic relationships.

Before I was born, my uncle Bubba got attacked by a couple of guys, and my father jumped in to help him. With strength like the Hulk, my father had a pretty good hold of one of the men, so much so that the guy's friend pulled out a gun and shot my father in the leg twice in an attempt to get him to release the man in his grip. A scenario like this would scare the average person, but instead it angered my father even more. Despite the apparent pain, he fought harder, beating the guy as the friend screamed for him to stop. Eventually the pain in his leg kicked in, and he loosened his grip, letting the guys run off.

Again, my father could've died that day, yet in his eyes, I imagine it would've been worth it, going out protecting his big brother.

The traditional roles of a father include being the protector, the provider, and the disciplinarian. I'll never meet my grandfather, but I feel like I know him. I see him in my father, in the traditions and traits he carried despite not spending a lot of time with him. My grandfather Rannell was murdered a week after my father's sixth birthday. Stabbed to death on the very street he called home, my grandfather left behind his wife and seven or eight children. He was only thirty-two years old when he passed. These are all things I recently learned from reconnecting with his family in Estill and combing through records online.

Although he lived a short life, my grandfather's memory and strength have lived on through his children and subsequent generations. Since my endometriosis diagnosis, I've wanted to know more about this side of the family, so initially I reached out to my dad to learn more about his father. Asking my father about sensitive topics, whether in person or over the phone, always makes me nervous, so I opted to send him a text instead: "Hey, Dad! Do you know if Grandpa had an obituary?" He responded right away that he wasn't sure, but he mentioned that it was possible my cousins Jeff or Jimmy Lee might have a copy, if it existed. Jeff, my grandfather's nephew who is now eighty-six, has dementia and was unlikely to be a reliable source, so I tried reaching out to Jimmy Lee via text message. He didn't have the obituary either, so I asked if he knew the exact date of Grandpa's passing so I could look online and get ahold of his death certificate. While he didn't know the date, he promised me he would look into it.

Jimmy Lee kept his word. No more than a day went by before I received a text that said, "He was born 1932, he was killed 1964. They had a funeral in Estill, SC. I will find out more. I believe he had seven or eight kids." I couldn't believe my grandfather lost his life at thirty-two years old. I had always known he died young, but it still felt like a shock. He had barely lived. Discovering his age fueled my curiosity even further. I needed his exact death date in order to obtain his death certificate.

I asked Jimmy Lee if he could find more information. Only ten minutes went by, and he sent me a photo of his application for a headstone, which my grandmother filled out. It contained the precise date of my grandfather's death, a detail unknown even to my father since he was so young at the time of his death.

A couple weeks went by, and I received an email from a cousin in Estill. Jimmy Lee told her I was looking for information on our family and she wanted to help. "Did you know that your great-grandmother had another girl that died. I have the death certificate. She was born April 2, 1930, and died May 22, 1930. I'll send you a copy of the certificate." This email was loaded and left me feeling hopeful that I would gain more insight soon, but I was also saddened by the thought of there being a baby who didn't survive. I wanted to know why she passed, what her name was, and if my great-grandmother had any health challenges while carrying her. I was learning so much, and I knew this was only the beginning.

I am grateful to my grandfather for giving me life. I believe if he could see any of us, or at least my father, he would be proud. My father lives his life in a way that honors my grandfather each day, never giving up on his children or his role as a parent and now grandparent to my niece and nephew. Yet, and still, I wonder how differently my father and his siblings would've turned out if they had grown up in a two-parent home. I wish they could've seen love through the relationship my grandfather and grandmother shared, a love that could've possibly saved her from years of sadness and pain, a love that might've even saved my parents' relationship.

I've yearned my entire life to know more about the man I've only ever seen one picture of. As his grandchild, who has been afforded more time on earth than he was, I can't help but think about how much he still had to learn and do in life. Now in my late thirties and welcoming my first child, I often reflect on how the violence inflicted upon my grandfather impacted not only his children but his grandchildren, leaving us all perpetually vigilant in a cruel and scary world.

I recently heard a quote that struck me hard: "Pain travels through families until someone is ready to feel it. For many of us, our generational curse is avoidance. We come from people who just act like it didn't happen, but pain demands to be felt. And somewhere down the line, a child will be born whose charge it is to feel it all." Violence, whether you're the aggressor or the receiver, has the potential to break families, homes, and spirits for generations.

As I meditated on my gratitude for my grandfather, I thought about the mothers whose children have been violently taken from them or the children who have lost parents to senseless acts of violence or abuse. How do they grieve and find the strength to pick up the pieces to move forward? How do they choose peace as their next steps? Perhaps their empathy is even bigger than my own understanding of what's possible.

> "We must understand people on both
> sides of the gun. They both need our help
> because hurt people hurt people."
>
> —Erica Ford

Victim Blaming

The universal silence surrounding violence stands out as a shared trait across communities, perhaps in an effort to protect the family's privacy and emotional well-being. This is especially prevalent when suicide occurs, and the reasons why are often whispered among small groups but rarely discussed openly. Families may prefer to keep the details of violent situations private to avoid public scrutiny, media attention, or the stigma associated with being a victim of crime. But there is no shame in being the victim of violence, and there is no room for blaming victims for their plight in life. In fact, in this state of victimhood, one can usually conjure up a new level of strength, resilience, and personal power.

Victim blaming occurs when the victim of any wrongful act is held entirely or partially at fault for the harm that was caused to them. It can happen in very loud and public ways, like in social media comments, allowing the wrongdoer the opportunity to avoid accountability. It also happens in less obvious ways when people ask seemingly innocent questions to get to the root of whether or not someone encouraged the actions that took place, like when a family member questions a victim's intention for telling their truth. Victim blaming has played a major role in explaining away various types of abuse, especially against women and children.

Aside from the fear of not being believed or being victim blamed, there are other more apparent reasons why a victim would choose silence. These include shame, fear of retaliation, or a reluctance to relive the trauma. These are all valid reasons for why someone who has been harmed would decide not to report an incident or speak openly about it with others. On the other end, attackers or aggressors often stay quiet about their transgressions due to potential judgment, punishment, or guilt. Then there are witnesses, those who remain silent because they've been asked to or because they feel it's not their story to tell. This collective silence creates a cycle in which the true extent of violence within families is rarely acknowledged or addressed, perpetuating a culture of denial and generations of secrecy and lingering pain.

Home should be a safe space, a place that, no matter the location, protects everyone from harm. A "safe space" is not a mere announcement; it's a conclusion based on the intentionality of all parties and the potential for repairing any conflict that arises. But the sanctity of a home is shattered when the very people who are supposed to protect you become the perpetrators of violence against you. This betrayal of trust can have life-long effects, destroying the sense of psychological safety and security that every individual is entitled to.

Growing up I saw many suspicious things, especially during my trips to the South. I was still pretty naive at the time and didn't fully understand what was going on, so I only learned about the harsh realities of some of my cousins being preyed upon by sexual predators when I became an adult, and they were ready to talk about it. I wish I could've protected them, and even now, I wish there was a way to hold those people accountable, but they're no longer with us. My very strict father did everything he could to ensure I was always in a safe place, and because of that I didn't go to sleepovers or hang out at strangers' homes. He also kept me away from company that would come over to drink and party, often sending me to my room to be in a "child's place." Back then I was annoyed by this, but today, I am grateful.

Do you know if any of the women or children in your family have experienced sexual violence at the hands of another family member? According to a recent study published by the National Sexual Violence Resource Center, 91 percent of victims of rape and sexual assault are female, and 9 percent are male. More alarming is the fact that in eight out of ten cases of rape, the victim knew the person who sexually assaulted them. One in four girls and one in six boys will be sexually abused before they turn eighteen years old, and 34 percent of people who sexually abuse a child are family members.[1] These statistics are not just numbers; they represent real people and untold stories of suffering within what should be the safest of environments.

As a society, we must foster an environment where victims feel safe to come forward without fear of judgment or retaliation. We should welcome others to tell their truths, whether they come forward immediately or thirty years after the fact. The truth, although at times ugly, should be honored. That's how we get to a place of openness and trust. Supporting survivors, promoting awareness, and implementing preventive measures can help break the cycle of abuse in and out of the home and heal families that have lived through generations of painful secrets. With collective action and empathy, healing and safety are possible for all parties.

Responding to and supporting victims of violence requires a compassionate and multifaceted approach. Open and empathetic discussions that provide a safe space for victims to share their experiences are crucial. In these conversations it's important to act as an ally, listening first and then encouraging healing and accountability. If a family member or friend is disclosing a violent experience, RAINN's National Sexual Assault Hotline staff suggests you respond with something like, "I believe you. It took a lot of courage to tell me this."

Victims of intimate partner violence or sexual abuse have diverse needs that are often influenced by the severity of their attack and its consequences. When someone you love is brave enough to share this type of experience, it's less important to offer advice as it is to offer resources and recommend service providers like legal assistance, counseling, and others who can assist with safety support. You should also encourage them to seek medical attention, both physical and mental, if needed. These responses encourage healing and provide options, even if your loved ones don't choose to take advantage of them right away.

Post-Traumatic Slave Disorder

Black people are not inherently violent, but in America, many have PTSD from the violence that was imposed upon us for centuries. I believe it's the same for descendants of the Holocaust, the Trail of Tears, and countless other groups that have been harmed by centuries of colonization, war, and displacement. The painful memories of these events live within us, whether we experienced them ourselves or not, so when we're triggered, we are going to fight back; we'll go straight into survival mode. I've had the honor of studying African-American Multigenerational Trauma and Implementing Models of Change under Dr. Joy Degruy, a well-known author and educator. Dr. Degruy studied slavery as a long-enduring trauma and speaks often about her theory of PTSD, post-traumatic slave disorder, the multigenerational trauma that descendants of the Transatlantic Slave Trade are left to contend with today.

Many people believe this theory is outdated, suggesting that African Americans no longer experience suffering or unfair treatment, but Dr. Degruy's research shows us the opposite. Even generations who have never witnessed a lynching or stepped foot on a plantation can physically feel the pain of slavery. And I have personally observed the manifestations of Dr. DeGruy's theory within my community. Here are a few issues that are prevalent among Black people, which, in my view, align perfectly with Dr. Degruy's form of PTSD:

- **ADULTS WHO BELIEVE THEY WILL DIE YOUNG:** These people don't see long lives for themselves because they've been exposed to so much death around them that a long life seems unattainable.

- **PEOPLE LIVING WITH SURVIVOR'S GUILT:** Survivor's guilt is a condition where individuals feel guilty for surviving a traumatic event when others did not. It is intertwined with the complex legacy of slavery and ongoing systemic injustices, and it reveals the psychological burden of outliving peers who have succumbed to violence, incarceration, or other systemic failures.

- **ISSUES WITH AMERICA'S PRISON SYSTEM:** In the US, many policies have significantly contributed to the disproportionate incarceration of Black individuals. The War on Drugs initiated in the 1970s targeted Black and other marginalized communities despite similar drug usage rates in white communities, often giving harsher sentences for drugs more commonly used by Black people. Stop and frisk policies also allowed for disproportionate targeting of Black and Latino communities, leading to higher arrest rates for minor offenses. And the school-to-prison pipeline, characterized by zero-tolerance policies in schools, disproportionately funnel Black and Latino students into the criminal justice system. Collectively, these policies have not only increased the incarceration rates among Black Americans but have also perpetuated cycles of trauma and disadvantage within these communities that have been working to build a fair and just life for themselves and their families since the Thirteenth Amendment was passed and we were declared "free."

- **THE IMPACT OF BROKEN FAMILIES:** This situation, never intended by us, persists due to the legacy of slavery, which leaned heavily on the forced separation and disruption of the Black familial structure. This historical disruption still impacts the cohesion and stability of Black families today, leading to enduring financial and relational challenges. Moreover, a significant number of children of color, particularly Black children, find themselves in the foster care system, which further reflects the ongoing struggles our people face against systemic barriers to family unity and support.

- **HURT PEOPLE HURT PEOPLE:** This phrase captures the ongoing cycle of trauma and violence in communities marked by generational abuse and neglect. It highlights how unresolved pain and suffering can escalate into further harm or retaliation within the community that could have easily been prevented. This statement also holds true due to displaced anger. This is why healing ourselves through therapy when we're hurting or grieving is so important.

Questions for Your Family

I encourage you to take the time to initiate a conversation about violence within your home. It doesn't have to be about a particular incident, nor do you have to call out any specific individuals, but it's important we begin talking about violence and see what we learn about ourselves and others. You can use the following conversation starters or ask the questions that have been on your mind.

- In your opinion, is there a cycle of violence happening within our family?

- What type of violence did you witness the most growing up?

- Are there any places where you feel unsafe?

- Who do you feel the need to protect the most in our family? And why?

- In what ways do you believe we, as a family, can contribute to reducing violence in our community?

After speaking with your family, journal about what you learned. Write about the current injustices you're experiencing at home and in your community, and include your family's views and responses. Future generations will thank you for the insight.

While many of us wish we could go back in time and relive situations differently or save those we love the most, we don't have that power. What we do have is an absolute right to create a more just world and tackle the issues that have negatively impacted us so they don't continue to harm future generations. We have the right to empathize and allow people the space to be heard. We also have the right to fight for justice.

Living in a constant state of anxiety or hypervigilance is exhausting. That's why it's important to find the people and safe spaces within and outside of your family that allow you to rest. It took me nearly my entire life to prioritize this, with my husband calling attention to the absurdity of some of my ideas. Living in fear isn't fair or normal. The coping mechanisms we accumulate throughout life in response to this fear are normal, and in general, coping is necessary to stay well. This is why my therapist always reminds me to continuously discover new coping strategies. As I've been working through healing for my grandfather and healing from the abuse and harm against my family and ancestors, I've leaned more heavily on some techniques than others.

Five Tips for Coping with Post-Traumatic Stress of All Kinds

1. **GET PHYSICALLY ACTIVE:** Getting up and moving your body doesn't have to only look like going to the gym. Exercise can be dancing, going for a hike, attending self-defense classes, taking brisk walks, or engaging in any physical movement that feels good to your body. It can also be a great way to blow off some steam.

2. **TAP INTO YOUR CREATIVITY:** Activities like designing, drawing, writing, making music, or inventing something new can be therapeutic for some people. Use your emotions as inspiration to create.

3. **LEAN IN WITH THOSE YOU LOVE:** Some of the best comfort comes from those we hold close to us. Sharing your experiences, feelings, and fears with people you trust can help you feel less isolated and more understood. I do this in a variety of ways, like introducing weekly thought-provoking questions in my group chats, telling my loved ones how much they mean to me, and showing up to support people in ways I'd want to feel supported.

4. **VOLUNTEER OR DO SELFLESS ACTS OF SERVICE:** Every day is a chance to do something good for the world. Giving back and making time to help people can be incredibly rewarding for someone dealing with post-traumatic stress. Volunteering provides a sense of purpose and can help you build connections with the outside world and people who need support, just like you.

5. **TELL STORIES (OF COURSE!):** Your story doesn't have to be broadcast to the world, but it should be shared in some form or another. Storytelling allows individuals to process and share their experiences in a structured way and helps

people recall memories and important information that's needed to heal. It can also be a powerful method for making sense of what has happened in our lives. When we own our stories, we gain mental clarity, and we reduce the stigma and power of traumatic memories.

Questions for Yourself

Take a few moments to reflect on the following questions:

- Do I have any specific triggers that increase the likelihood that I will act aggressively or violently toward others?

- Is there anyone who deserves my forgiveness or distance for the violence they've caused against me?

- Moving forward, how can I heal my nervous system and protect myself from the impact of past violence?

- Am I choosing violence in any areas of my life?

After learning more about my grandfather's passing, I reached out to share everything I had gathered with my father. Surprisingly he was receptive and grateful to learn. I felt as though I was giving him some closure and allowing him to have space to talk freely about his father, which is something I had never seen him do. I was also able to share information with my cousins who have children that will grow up one day and become curious about who they are and how the world has shaped them and their ancestors. Violence has rocked my family in many ways, but we're learning through each generation how to stand up to it and respond accordingly.

Healer's Recap

- Living in a constant state of fear will take a toll on your mental health.

- You deserve to feel at ease.

- We must foster an environment where victims feel safe to come forward without fear of judgment or retaliation.

- Act as an ally to victims of violence by listening first, then encouraging healing and accountability.

- Hurt people don't have to hurt people.

- Continuously seek healthy coping strategies to manage grief, anger, or any feelings connected to the violence you've experienced.

- Encourage conversation at home about the violence in your family and community.

- Decide what cycle of violence will stop with you and future generations!

Chapter Eight

Coping in Silence

Can you name someone in your family who is seemingly silent as an act of self-preservation?

Engaging in silence isn't merely a matter of deciding whether to speak up or remain quiet. As I journeyed through my family's stories and opened the floor for new conversations, I hoped my family wouldn't see my desires for conversation as a mere binary choice. With deep reflection, I've come to understand that silence, whether in grief, relationships, or community, is often a result of external factors that can lead one to make an unconscious decision to seek peace instead of the pain of speaking up.

To my complete surprise, I received a package in the mail nearly eight months after I began asking my family members serious questions and searching for answers. Along with a package full of death certificates and ancestry findings that left me confused and slightly concerned, Jimmy Lee's sister also sent a note: "I guess you thought I have forgotten about you. Well, I haven't. I just need to take a break. I got overwhelmed. I thought your great-grandma had nine children; boy was I wrong. In the process of doing a tree, still researching the Russell family and looking for information about your grandfather."

From this box of ancestral knowledge, it turns out my grandmother had a few children who passed a month to a year and even a couple of years after their birth. How did this happen and why? Were they denied health care? Is there a more serious issue I should be aware of that runs in the family? Seeing this information with my very own eyes and preparing to give birth to my first child gave me both a rush of fear and the inspiration to keep going. There was a lot more to learn.

Silence in Grief

While I often observed silent tears with my mother, there are specific times I can recall myself and other family members doing the same during our times of grief. I've gone to funerals that have been so painful I could barely gasp for air. I felt as if I was falling apart, with nothing but sorrowful cries to contribute to the occasion. When I lost my first best friend, Troy, in a car accident at the age of thirty-five, I felt an unbearable pain, especially considering his son had died as well. At his funeral, when the opportunity arose to share memories, I knew my knees wouldn't be strong enough to make it up to the pulpit, so I sat in my pew and crumbled to pieces in my friend's arms. After the intensity of the emotions had passed a few weeks later, I wished I could've shared. If I could go back and grieve differently, I would've talked about how amazing of a friend he was to me and how my life had changed immensely because of everything I learned from him. My grief swallowed me; it felt like a physical barrier.

Understanding human behavior and even my own actions during moments of pain has taken extensive research and reflection. I was curious to find when and where people intentionally choose silence. In his article "What Is the Difference Between Quiet and Silence?" Joshua Gibbs shared an interesting take: "Quiet and silence have entirely different aims. We are quiet for the benefit of others, so as not to disturb them, but we are silent for the benefit of our souls. Silence is the undisturbing of the psyche."[1] This perspective was completely aligned with how I showed up at Uncle Bubba and Grandma Geri's funerals and I'm sure many other aspects of my life.

When my grandma G passed, I sat next to my mother and gripped her hand, trying to give her some of my strength to endure the entire ceremony without falling apart. When my Uncle Bubba passed, I wanted to be strong for my brother, who shed many tears, which is something I'd hardly ever seen. When the moment came to share reflections, I purposely chose to be quiet. I knew that more comfort could be given by being physically present for my loved ones rather than speaking words. I was able to read the room and focus on the biggest need.

In reflecting on these moments, I began to wonder what my father would have said if he had spoken at his father's funeral. It's a question I'm still afraid to ask him, but I wish to do so badly. Although he was a young boy at the time, I wish he could tap back into those emotions and share what he went through. I wondered if he could fully grasp what happened or if he still struggles to put his feelings into words. In an attempt to figure out the best way to engage in deep conversation with my father, I've thought about pretending it's not my question but something I've found in a game, like "What's something you would say at your parents' funerals?" Regardless, the question doesn't feel right passing my lips just yet, but my curiosity surrounding my father's inner world still encompasses me.

There's no right or wrong way to cope with death. Some people need to pause in reflection and focus within to process what they're feeling. When faced with significant chaos and pain, this is often our way of lessening the psychological impacts. In silence we can also build self-awareness and allow our thoughts to come and go as needed. It can allow for a beautiful opportunity for us to tap into moments that were temporarily forgotten, like past experiences that were buried with our busyness. When someone passes, we tend to think about how we experienced them in a way that absolutely no one else can relate to. It's natural and normal to allow for moments of silence. Temporarily remaining silent and embracing stillness is a powerful tool for healing, allowing us access to the part of our nervous system that eases our body's stress signals. And similarly, quietly sitting next to a friend or offering a hug is sometimes needed to give others space and support to process their thoughts and feelings before sharing them with the world. As a child, I often embraced the quiet to provide the peace and space I observed was needed by others.

When my grandma G passed away, I was about twenty years old. It was then, for the first time, I saw my father cry. The sight of him, a figure of strength and resilience in my eyes, vulnerably expressing sorrow struck me deeply. I had never before witnessed him in such a state of emotional rawness. I knew how much he loved my mother and her family, despite their divorce, and Grandma G had been a strong maternal figure for him. I wanted to comfort my dad, but as he turned his back to hide his face, I could feel he needed to process his grief in solitude, so I gave him space. I was afraid my words would frustrate him rather than provide comfort.

Have you ever needed to respect someone's need to cope in silence? The awareness and acknowledgment of their individual process of healing and grief is so important. When we force people to articulate their feelings before they are ready, it can inadvertently cause further emotional distress and distance between us and them, reinforcing feelings of isolation. Intuitively I knew that a key distinction between recognizing when it's time to encourage conversation and when it's time to allow for silence lies in empathy and attentive observation. When a person is ready to talk, they might show you through subtle signs of opening up, like asking for company or initiating conversations about unrelated matters. In contrast, signs that someone may not be ready to talk can look like short or one-word answers, withdrawal or distractive behaviors, a clear preference for solitude, or direct statements of wanting to be left alone. By creating a safe and accepting environment where people can open up in their own time, we nurture a foundation of trust and empathy. This is something I believe I've worked hard to do while also occasionally pushing slightly with questions that test whether or not the person is ready.

If a person isn't willing to talk, give them space and respect it. By doing this, you'll gain more of their trust and access to their vulnerability. Granting this grace doesn't mean we should always put our needs second, but rather, we should assess the urgency of the conversation or topic at hand. If the matter isn't immediate, it's often best to let it go for the time being. Forcing an issue before someone is ready to discuss it can do more harm than good, potentially damaging the trust and rapport you've worked to build. But what if the person never shows signs of wanting to open up? This is a valid question as well. I would suggest letting them know that you'll be there to talk when they're ready and continue to check in periodically. If you are concerned about their well-being, consider suggesting a therapist or local counselor who specializes in their category of trauma.

Silence in Relationships

There are situations where temporary silence can be a positive, and then there are times when people choose silence for their own convenience, even though it may have a negative impact on others. Have you ever chosen not to engage with someone in order to avoid a conversation or ignore an issue? Uncomfortable conversations can give people anxiety, and addressing truths can often force people into hiding. If you've ever experienced the end of a friendship where the friend simply unfollows you and goes silent or a relationship ends because they ghosted you without explanation, then you know this tactic all too well. Oftentimes these are people who find it easier to disappear rather than confront the problem. Unfortunately, in these situations, even if you want to connect and get answers, that doesn't mean that's what they feel is necessarily best for them. It's not easy to understand why people go into hiding, leaving you unsure if they ever cared, but it's important not to take this personally.

You don't truly know how someone is coping or what they're dealing with unless they tell you. We can assume based on what's happened in the past, but there's no way of knowing whether or not a person has strategies they practice in private. For all I know, the Russell side of my family could be engaging in various forms of self-care or therapeutic practices behind closed doors instead of speaking with others. And your family members could be praying, meditating, journaling, or even speaking with a therapist. Without initiating a conversation to uncover these details, we're merely speculating about their well-being and behaviors, potentially overlooking the depth and complexity of their coping mechanisms.

In times of anger or disagreement, I ask myself if I'm capable of delivering my feelings in a constructive way or if my tone will lean toward confrontation. I pause in this space of reflection and sometimes sleep on it or draft a text in my notes before confronting an issue. While taking this journey of total healing and familial understanding, I've had to be very delicate with my approach. Would you consider yourself easy to talk to? How do you react to other people's ideas or feelings that you disagree with or don't understand? While considering that some people may lean away from you because they are actively choosing isolation, we always have to make attempts to show up in ways that make people feel comfortable coming to us. Simple statements like, "I'm here" or "Call me if you ever need to talk," go such a long way, and responding, even if delayed, always makes a difference.

Coping in Community

When you open the door for dialogue, you'll quickly learn who is ready to lean in and who isn't. In my journey, I've grown closer to the family members who see the shared value in collecting family stories and history. I even started a group chat with my brother and two of my immediate cousins, Kisha and Rannell III (Uncle Bubba's kids). I decided I would share my learnings with them so they could have this information to pass on to their children one day. My brother rarely responds to texts, so he didn't reply to my initial message, but Rannell expressed gratitude and had questions, and Kisha responded by sharing her findings, some of which she had never previously shared.

One time Kisha went to my aunt's house and took photos of all the family obituaries in her collection. She flooded the group chat with photo after photo of black-and-white obituaries. Among these, she had collected several from my grandfather's siblings, and she had one I had been hoping for: the obituary of my great-grandmother, Grandma Catherine "Dee Dee" Russell. Her birthday was not recorded on her obituary, but I was able to gather that she was born sometime between 1895 and 1907. About thirty-five years before my great-grandmother was born, the census showed that 45.8 percent of white families in the state of South Carolina owned slaves. It's fair to assume that when my great-grandmother was born, as racial tensions escalated, the values and attitudes of white Americans were still deeply rooted in the ideologies of slavery, delaying African Americans the opportunity to find or use their voice.

White Americans resorted to lynching and other violent tactics, not only as a means of instilling fear but also to maintain control. According to the film *The Black Press: Soldiers Without Swords*, between the years 1882 and 1919, nearly 3,000 African Americans were murdered by lynch mobs. This means an African American was murdered every four and a half days. These murders were often celebrated among white communities and went unreported in mainstream media. Imagine how often the grieving families and communities resorted to silence to cope. To speak out or use your voice in any way in those times meant literally risking your life. This history alone helps me understand that while I try to process my family's preference to cope in silence, there's no reason to point blame at any of them for living like their ancestors. Breaking the cycle came with risks, and it still does.

From my great-grandmother's obituary, I learned that she passed away in 1979. Her obituary began with a faith statement, something that didn't surprise me at all seeing as her daughter, my aunt Genny, was partly responsible for teaching me about God. "We belong to God, not only for a few fleeting years we call life, but for eternity." The obituary told me how involved my great-grandmother Catherine was in the church, and how she even helped build a new one, which I assume is the one that hosted her funeral. Later learning that she had children to grieve, I felt a sense of appreciation that she had a church home to help her navigate those difficult times.

My great-grandmother and her husband Benny had nine children (or so I thought); her obituary named them—at least the ones people were aware of. With this information, I was able to do additional digging, finding some of their obituaries and seeing pictures of some of them for the very first time. Something that stood out to me was that all of the funerals were held at the same church in Estill, South Carolina.

Having information to share with my dad made it a bit easier to initiate conversations. Instead of prying with intrusive questions, I could be open with my findings and see if he was receptive. I started calling my father on his days off, typically in the early evening hours after he had finished his projects for the day and was starting to relax. "Hey, Dad, I found out so much today," I shared. He seemed excited by my findings. I hoped that by telling him about important dates and some parts of his family story, he would feel more connected to those he had lost and might respond with new information or ideas he hadn't previously shared. Our calls were short, but it was progress, and I felt pride in being able to offer my father something so priceless.

Surprisingly as time went on, my father began to open up in ways he'd never opened up before. On a few occasions he has called to volunteer information about his childhood, tell stories of things he's overcome, and share more about my great-grandparents. It seemed as though my sensitive approach worked and created an invitation that my father had always been waiting for. Seeing him in this new light inspired me to revisit some of the questions I was holding for him.

Prepare for Conversations with Therapy

I turned to my therapist for advice regarding ways to approach uncomfortable topics with loved ones. In the beginning I asked her, "How do you frame your questions in a way to get people to open up and not shut down?" She told me, "People open up when they feel safe, even when their instinct is to shut down. Feeling safe in a conversation helps them push through the discomfort. I use open-ended questions to get people to share. I may also frame it using language that connects to the person. It's not just about the question but the tone, timing, and context of how I set up the questions as well."

I paused and asked, "So how do I respond when they express verbally or nonverbally that they aren't ready to talk?" She shared, "I give them their space but let them know my intention in wanting to talk about a certain topic. I may share that I will come back to it at another time so they have more time to mentally prepare. I know there is fear and discomfort about opening up, so I will reassure my clients that I am sensitive to how challenging opening up is for them. I do not shut down or back away because someone isn't ready to talk. My role is about gently challenging and helping people get unstuck."

After our discussion, I sat with that word, "unstuck." Has my father been stuck all of these years? Or was it that I was stuck in our silence, feeling less connected and confused by what was being left unsaid? That night, I wrote out three questions for my father, then rewrote them about five times until I narrowed them down to a question that I thought would make him feel most comfortable.

1. I changed "How do you cope with grief?" to "How do you cope with loss?" Then I changed the word "cope" to ensure he would understand what I was asking: "What do you do to find comfort or peace after losing a loved one?"

2. I changed "What is something you want future generations to know about your dad?" to "What is something you want your grandkids to know about your dad?" My father is the ultimate "pop pop," and he's continuously thinking about the needs of his grandchildren. I figured if there was anyone he wanted to take pride in their roots, it was them.

3. Finally, I changed "What advice would you give me to cope with your loss one day?" to "One day, I may need to learn how to live without you. What advice do you have for future me to deal with the loss of you or mom?" Here, I also removed the word "cope" and rearranged the question to one in which my father could imagine the scenario a bit better.

Sunday came around and I wanted to speak with my dad, but basketball games were on TV that day, so I knew my chances were slim. I wasn't sure if I should wait and call during a commercial or text him and give him the option to call me when he was ready. I decided on a text: "Dad, can I ask you three hard questions?" The familiar flutter of childhood nerves nearly took over me, but I hit send. Two minutes later, when commercials came on, he called.

"What's up, Cole?" He responded in good spirits. The ball was in my court. I launched into my questions, not in the sequence I had planned, but led by spontaneity. I decided to start with the question that came to me on the spot.

"Dad, I'm writing about grief, and I have a few tough questions for you. The first is one day you will pass, and I'll need to write your obituary. Who on earth knows the most about you?"

Without hesitation, he answered, "Jimmy Lee." I wasn't surprised by this answer as he was the one person my father spoke to most often, and the duo had known each other their entire lives.

I moved on to the next question while blending two questions in one, "What advice would you give me to cope with your loss one day, and how do you find peace with loss?"

His advice was heartfelt and simple. "You find peace when you are around people and talk about the person as much as you can. Good times or bad. Whatever you have to share. Being by yourself is not good. Share all the good times so people know the stories." His response was not just advice but a revelation to me. It made me realize that perhaps my father had been navigating his own path to healing all this time, only silently and unseen by me.

During the conversation my father seemed calm and open, so I continued with my questioning. "What is something you want your grandkids to know about your dad?"

His response was fast, "Without him, there wouldn't be us!" Then he took a beat. "He was smart. He was a person that could do anything, fix anything, and could even build a house. He was so good with his hands. At least that's what everyone would tell me about him. I think I inherited some of that, but I also taught myself a bit. I watched different people who would fix things and asked questions. I was very curious because I wanted to know how to do all of those things too."

My father has raised me into the woman I am today and has been able to see my growth in every way. On this day, however, when I spoke to him, I could feel his growth as well. He was so open with me, and I realized I was completely wrong about how he'd react to my questions and attempts to get closer to him through his answers. After I asked my questions, we began freely talking about the church that had conducted the funerals for all of his relatives in Estill, South Carolina. I needed to unlearn who my father used to be and allow this new version to continue healing and speaking.

Silent Coping Strategies Are Not Permanent Decisions

The more my father shared, the more I realized I shouldn't be afraid or discouraged by one's silence because it's a state that doesn't have to last forever. Sometimes parents choose not to share or acknowledge their pain with their young children. This decision can stem from a desire to protect their children from the complexities and burdens of adult emotions and problems. This is something I believe my father learned from his grieving mother. I never witnessed Grandma Rose express vulnerability through her emotions. She was always too busy being strong. And my father, who appeared to quietly cope with challenges, was likely shielding me from the harsher realities of life and coping in ways that simply weren't obvious to me. It seemed to be a generational approach.

In the book *The Handbook of Child Psychology*, William Damon and Richard M. Lerner suggest that exposing children to adult issues too early can cause anxiety, confusion, and emotional distress. Regardless of race, it's recommended to provide age-appropriate information to avoid overwhelming your child with the complexities and challenges of adulthood too soon.[2] With this in mind, it's understandable why a parent might not cry to their child with the news of a sudden death or talk to them about end-of-life planning, mental distress, serious situations, or pain. These types of protective instincts are rooted in our desire to preserve the innocence and emotional well-being of our offspring.

The challenge for the adult child then becomes, How do I catch up on what I missed? How can I get my parents to tell me about the things they didn't feel were appropriate to share with me because I was possibly too young to understand or perhaps because they didn't want me to see them in a different light? Entering this phase of craving deeper conversation requires the adult child to take the initiative, signaling to their parents their readiness to handle complex, mature topics. Despite forever being seen as their parents' child, it's crucial for the adult child to demonstrate their growth and capacity for understanding. For example, I learned that my little sister was ready for adult conversation when she started inquiring more about how I was feeling. She would lurk close to my door or quietly enter the room if she overheard me venting. She would offer unsolicited advice when she felt it would be helpful or sometimes just sit down and ask, "Are you okay?" I appreciated it so much, and eventually I became more comfortable opening up to her, realizing she too could relate to some of my stress.

Don't wait until a moment of frustration to tell your elders that you're ready for mature conversation. Consider approaching them delicately with something like "When you're ready, can we talk about what happened with (topic)?" or "I was wondering how I could find more information about (topic). Can you share anything with me?"

Four Healthy Coping Strategies Without Conversation for All Ages

Contrary to the overall theme of this book, conversations are not the only strategy for healing. There are plenty of silent ways to cope. When you see a loved one struggling to cope with a situation, you can offer certain activities to help soothe their nervous system and quiet their mind.

1. PAINT: In my work with the Precious Dreams Foundation, we introduce art therapy as a way of coping with difficult days. At home, it's something I started doing with my friends and loved ones. None of us are master painters, but we would sit around and make paintings according to different prompts to help us tap into different sides of ourselves.

Here are some of my favorite painting prompts for gathering with loved ones:

- Think of three words that give you peace. Merge them into a picture. Visualize this image. Now try to replicate it on the canvas.

- When you're feeling low, what do you need? Bring this vision to life on the canvas.

- If you could reimagine the sky, what colors would you see? Attempt to paint only the colors and elements that would give people comfort each day.

- What is your current vibe? Paint your feelings in a picture.

2. **CREATE A RELAXING SETTING:** Find what gives the person you love comfort and create that environment for them. This could be sitting around watching a basketball game, taking a boat ride, joining them for a nap on the couch, or simply going for a walk. Sign up to do something with your loved one that will take them to their comfort place.

3. **SUGGEST A DIGITAL DETOX:** Keeping up with the outside world can be mentally draining. Encourage your loved one to take a break from scrolling. Join them in detoxing from screens for a day or a week. This can help relieve them of the pressure to update others on what's happening in their lives and stop comparing their lives to what others are presenting online.

4. **LET MUSIC SPEAK FOR YOU:** Music can be so timeless, and a single song has the power to encapsulate the entirety of our emotions and experiences. Encourage your loved ones to listen to specific albums or curate a playlist for them. Music has the ability to draw out the battles

we've pushed into the shadows, stirring up memories, emotions, and sensations that might be too complex or overwhelming to articulate.

Questions for Yourself

It's easy to point the finger at who hasn't shared or who has chosen to remain silent. In this headspace, it's harder to show up with empathy and be a leader within your family to encourage people to share their stories and document them appropriately. With this in mind, take a few moments to ask yourself the following questions:

- With a better understanding of why people remain silent, has my perspective changed on anyone in my family?

- Has there been a time when I remained silent even though I had the opportunity to share? How do I feel reflecting on that moment today?

- Have I made a real effort to know both sides of the family and their history? If not, what's stopping me from learning, whether through research or conversation?

When we hide parts of our past, we drift away from our most authentic selves and history. Over time, we may find that we've given up little pieces of who we are to become someone the world can't break. If you reflect on who has hurt you or your loved ones, it will point you to the source of the issue so you can begin focusing on healing and reclaiming what was taken from you. In this space, you'll find a sense of awakening power you didn't realize you could ever have, a power to set boundaries that allows you to be soft yet respected.

Although emotionally reserved, my brave personality and approach to community care are most like my father's. That's likely because he raised me. There are behaviors and traits I've picked up along the way from watching him so closely. Born in the 1960s, my father grew up in a time when campaigns and policies were critically needed to help Black people achieve safety and basic rights. I often think about the March on Washington, the massive protest that captured the attention of the world, where Martin Luther King Jr. delivered his iconic "I Have a Dream" speech at the Lincoln Memorial. I think about my father being an elementary school student when the Voting Rights Act of 1965 was introduced, which aimed to overcome legal voting barriers for African Americans at the state and local levels. My father was born into a world that told him his voice didn't matter. That realization alone helps me understand why we have generations of silent people in our families. So many of our ancestors grew up around hate and discrimination and were taught to dislike their own skin, culture, and hair. With these reflections, it's clear why I must stand firm in my identity and utilize every right fought for by my ancestors.

I truly appreciate the many people of color forging the path of self-care, self-preservation, and self-love today. Their contributions have helped destigmatize mental health issues, promote healing practices, and create spaces where Black individuals can find the courage to be vulnerable, let their guard down, and finally receive the healing they need. It's because of their efforts, as well as the path my father and those before him paved, that I can be louder and more expressive than they were. Thanks to them, I have the freedom to speak.

Healer's Recap

- Engaging in silence isn't merely a matter of deciding whether to speak up or remain quiet.

- Temporarily remaining silent and embracing stillness is a powerful tool for healing, allowing access to the part of our nervous system that eases the body's stress signals.

- Silence is sometimes needed to give others the space they need to process their emotions.

- When someone is not ready to talk, they will show you.

- You don't truly know how someone is coping unless you ask.

- Don't be complacent with the silence of others. Encourage conversation and give your loved ones the opportunity to open up.

- Understand where silence was taught within your family and who it has impacted the most.

Part Three

Speak or Repeat

Chapter Nine

Silent Apologies

Have you ever wanted an apology from a family member that you know you'll never receive? How have you been able to move forward or are you still waiting?

When I think about the phrase "I'm sorry," I often wonder if my ancestors ever heard it from those who oppressed them, and even if they did, what would it mean? What would it teach them? And what were they learning about how and when apologies are necessary?

Acknowledging how we harm each other is necessary for human solidarity. Although it's become a controversial topic of whether or not you should apologize in certain situations, I believe that apologies show our humility, and there's something very admirable about a person who can consider how their actions impact others and admit their wrongdoing. This shouldn't be confused with over-apologizing, which can be a result of low self-esteem or self-worth. This is about making a sincere statement after deep reflection and acknowledging that you've wronged someone or caused them harm in some way.

I'm not a perfect communicator, but I certainly try to use words as a way to connect with myself and others. For as long as I could remember, I chose writing—whether it was music, children's books, or handwritten letters to friends that I would fold like an origami fortune teller and pass to friends between periods. I've always leaned into finding my voice and true expression through writing or typing it out.

On one particular evening, I sat to meditate and the word "apology" kept popping up. Unsure of who, what, or where to put my focus to begin dissecting it, I decided to open my journal for some free writing:

> I am my ancestors, humbly speaking
> I hold myself accountable to them
> I hold myself accountable for how I've mishandled people
> I release pain
> I hold myself accountable for how I've treated myself
> I release pain because the consequences of hiding it in
>   place are larger than the discomfort of confronting it
> I reject hate
> I reject hate because I see my enemies as humans
>   diverted from God's path
> I speak truth
> I speak truth for the little kid in me that carried loud
>   thoughts
> I apologize
> I apologize because that's the only way to create a fair future

Although they weren't physically free, I believe my ancestors lived free in their minds, and that's the hope they carried with them to face each day. Revisiting the painful experiences of my ancestors seems self-sabotaging in a sense, but I know that reflecting on their suffering releases it. When we look back, we give ourselves an opportunity to honor our past and become fully informed, allowing our reflections of the past to influence how we move forward. This alone promotes growth, allowing us to pass on knowledge, learn to forgive, and make fully informed decisions.

The benefits of looking back to move forward are well known. This is why in the beginning of forming a relationship with a psychotherapist, they'll likely inquire about your history to understand who you are today. Psychotherapy (also known as talk therapy) can be helpful in teaching you how to identify and change troubling emotions, thoughts, and behaviors that come from reflecting.[1] Understanding the link between your past and present is essential for healing, so when you find it hard to talk about your past, it might indicate there's an area that requires further exploration.

As I sat with the word "apology" and dissected my writing, I chose to focus on one particular line: "I hold myself accountable for how I've treated myself." I decided to list out everything I deserved an apology for. I listed the times I stayed in rooms too long where people did not value or respect my mind and body; I wrote out the names of people I felt wronged me but, in all honesty, showed me how much I lacked self-love; and I wrote about the dreams ignored, the things I told myself I wasn't smart enough to achieve. As these situations unfolded, I learned from them. I found the lesson, but then I moved on. I didn't do for myself the thing I would've wanted from others: I didn't apologize.

Questions for Yourself

Let's get right to it! In this reflection, I want you to point the finger back at yourself and uncover the ways in which you've allowed silence to mute parts of your story and character. I've looked back centuries in an effort to understand my family. Now, I'm creating the mental space to look back at the last ten to thirty years and reflect on what I've kept quiet. I encourage you to do the same by asking yourself the following questions:

- Do I owe myself an apology?

- Where have I let myself down?

- Am I holding myself back from enjoying life fully because of my past?

- Am I allowing time for inner dialogue and conversation with myself when reflecting on these questions? How much time feels right to me?

If you read these questions, gave them a quick thought, and then chose to keep reading even if you weren't content with your responses, you're not doing the work. Take a break and sit in what doesn't feel right with your spirit! The truth and the assignment will be revealed to you.

People who tend to move on quicker than others will tell you their mode of thinking is the easiest way to cope, but in reality, it's actually the hardest way to heal. The faster we move forward, the slower we feel, if ever. When we rush to move on without processing our feelings, we're practicing an unhealthy coping technique known as emotional avoidance. By bypassing this emotional processing phase, we prevent ourselves from learning the lessons that can come with each experience. It's so important we take our time confronting and understanding our feelings. If not, we leave scars of unresolved issues that can resurface in harmful ways and manifest as a cycle of repeated lessons.

In her book *Dare to Feel*, Alexandra Roxo says, "Controlling your feelings by numbing or silencing them creates a pattern inside of you that may go on your whole life. Denying your emotions and your felt sense of life is denying your reality."[2] When we move on from anything quickly, we are making the conscious decision to hit the light switch on our feelings. This is something I've done for years, never really focusing on this growth area until now. Today I have no interest in carrying emotional weight, whether intentionally or unintentionally. I'm finally giving myself the grace to reflect on the bad and give myself the energy and space to feel whatever comes from it and take accountability for it.

We All Make Mistakes

The greatest leaders are those who can admit when they've made a mistake. They understand the importance of building self-awareness and holding themselves accountable for their daily decisions. In more recent years, I've begun to fear there will be a generation of people who don't keep their word, a generation of people who say whatever they want and reject consequences because they're lying to themselves about the impact of their decisions. It's easy to create a different version of ourselves that can live in alternate realities or online, but at the end of the day, we're still left with reality, no matter where we focus most of our time. The real you needs check-ins every now and then. It needs you to remember that the most important character you can build is the one that is real. And if you're struggling with holding yourself accountable, you can always allow others to. People's opinions are not facts, but I encourage you to invite those close to you to share their honest opinions, and try your absolute best to listen and not become defensive.

A culture has been created in today's world where people believe avoidance behavior is a technique for wellness. But ghosting people, silencing those who speak out, and constantly running from problems are unhealthy ways of managing relationships. Even in situations where we need to cut ties or part ways with family and friends, we can do so in a way that allows for reflection, respect, and sharing before the relationship comes to an end. While we have the ability to control our feelings, and I believe we absolutely should sometimes, we can't forget that growth results from feeling, reflecting, and taking steps forward with absolute acceptance of the truth.

Nicole

In my work I provide comfort to people in their most vulnerable moments, but in my personal life I can't afford to give everyone that luxury. Setting boundaries and protecting my nervous system has offended many people throughout my life, whether it was family, friends, or romantic suitors. With no regrets, I can reflect on those situations and wish the best for those I've had to release in order to flourish. Yet, I also acknowledge that my tendency to quickly let go may have inadvertently hindered the other person's healing process.

I used to be the person to let a friend or lover go with just one text, email, or phone call, wrapping things up quickly without truly giving people the opportunity to engage in a back-and-forth dialogue. Once I got to a point of being fed up, lingering in the energy of an unhealthy situation wasn't worth it for me, not even for a ten-minute conversation.

I used my silence as a weapon and distance as a punishment instead of talking it through or giving the other person the opportunity to correct their behavior. Seems unfair, right? This is because I often gave people second and third chances in my mind, but never truly communicated with them that their mishandling of our relationship would lead to these types of consequences. It was a buildup of issues for me but not necessarily for them. For this, I'm absolutely sure there are people who are likely sitting somewhere waiting for an apology from me.

I love to see the good in people. I'm the friend who will see others' mistakes as a teaching moment, forgetting that God most likely didn't assign me to be the teacher in every situation. In the past, I would question my intuition, making excuses for long-term friends or family members because of their past traumas. I would do anything to avoid confrontation. One of my biggest triggers stems from watching my father's family yell and argue with each other as a child, so I don't like when people raise their voices, I don't like arguing, and peace for me used to mean absolutely no drama.

In the past, I felt comfortable speaking up at home but not in my external relationships. I'd allow myself to experience a buildup of let-downs or confirmations that certain people didn't deserve space in my world. I discovered that the longer I neglected my feelings for external peace, the more I wanted to end the relationship, rather than talk about their transgressions. In their eyes perhaps, I went from kind and empathetic to cold and guarded. Although my feelings were validated in my mind, perhaps they weren't completely understood by the person who was released from my life with little to no warning. Perhaps they deserved to know they were losing me before it was too late.

Shortly after my parents' separation, I remember my grandmother Rose and my aunts sitting around the table talking negatively about my mom. At just eight years old, it angered me to sit there and hear people tear down my favorite woman in the world. I said nothing at the moment, but I remember sitting at the top of the stairs in tears, wishing I could defend her. As soon as I went home, I told my mom everything I'd heard. I was angry and so was my mother. I remember her saying, "You don't have to go over there anymore." As much as I knew my mother made that statement out of anger, she followed it up with a lesson about protecting my energy by distancing myself from negative people, and she made visiting grandma optional. Never would I have thought this could apply to people as close to me as my father's mother and his sisters. I started to view family differently at that point. I knew that no matter who it was, I needed to feel comfortable and respected in order to be in their presence. While I never stopped visiting my grandmother, I took this mentality with me everywhere, creating boundaries with everyone I encountered.

Before I met my husband, my uncle Derek sat me down and shared his concerns about my tendency to date "men with a broken wing." I had never categorized my exes in that way, but he was right. Every ex needed support in some way, whether with their mental health, career, lifestyle, or financial situation. My desire to help others would always leak into these romantic relationships.

Growing up living in a home with a single father, I saw him struggle to manage the house and finances on his own. It developed a strong compassion in me toward devoted fathers, and interestingly, that compassion extended into one of my relationships. At one point I moved in with a partner to help him financially after he lost a job. He had a daughter, and it pained me to see how difficult it was for him to be in a position where he couldn't provide for her. Yet, after moving in, my intuition began to tell me that he was not a great partner. His misery from unemployment took over every part of his life, and I no longer felt appreciated or loved in the ways I knew I deserved. On our first Christmas Eve together, I stayed up and wrapped his daughter's gifts in our bedroom while he slept five feet away, snoring the night away. I processed that moment as perhaps him finding difficulty in accepting that he couldn't afford the gifts under the tree and he had to accept help. Despite my disappointment, it wasn't a deal breaker.

Then one day I got into a car accident, and suddenly I couldn't provide. I was working fewer hours and could no longer hold down the household chores, food shopping, and daily cooking. Each day, I dealt with excruciating back pain, and when I needed him most, I realized our support was not mutual. That summer, while recovering in physical therapy, I would go to bed early so I could be alone to cry myself to sleep. I was overwhelmed by both physical and emotional pain, while he was usually in the living room drinking away his sorrows. At no point did he offer any support or ask if I'd had something to eat throughout the day. Being the only full-time worker in the home, I had to recover from my accident with no empathy from my partner, and the resentment built fast.

One day I stumbled upon a receipt tucked away in our shared closet for a deposit on an engagement ring. It scared the crap out of me. How could he afford a ring when he couldn't afford the rent? I knew then he was not my person, and I almost felt as if an engagement would be a trap. I would be stuck in this cycle of disappointment with a person who didn't value me or my contributions. I returned the receipt to its original spot and acted as though I had never seen it. After a couple of days went by and I was able to fully comprehend the possible outcomes if he were to propose, I decided to look for apartments and plan an escape. I ended the relationship and told him I was moving out all at once. While I'm confident that I complained from time to time, once I got to my breaking point, there wasn't much to explain. And rightfully so, I was not going to stay in any environment where I didn't feel comfortable or valued. Yet this pattern of spontaneously unloading and leaving highlighted a deeper issue within my approach to relationships.

Although I grew up craving conversation, it didn't mean I knew how to do it. Would I have experienced different outcomes if I could confront people at the first sight of red flags? Would he have thought about engagement if I didn't pretend to be so understanding and passive? It took years of therapy and disappointment to understand how to even approach people to discuss conflict, and whenever someone approached me to discuss an issue, I would quickly apologize and hope that they would accept it and move on. It took time for me to grow comfortable talking about feelings in my personal life.

Desperately trying to find my identity in my twenties, I learned that I needed to find the balance between offering support to others and ensuring my own needs were met. It was a realization that required me to look back and analyze my relationships and my approach to conflict. Why was I proud to say I would give someone the coat off my back? Why did I attract men and friends with "broken wings"? Did I have a longing to feel needed, or did I find some selfish enjoyment underneath it all by being a fixer? Delving deeper, I began to understand that this tendency might have stemmed from my childhood, where I often found myself being sensitive and considerate of everyone's energy and actions. The little girl in me who tiptoed around the house grew up to tiptoe around her relationships until she was ready to go. This role that I continued to play well into adulthood taught me to prioritize the needs of others above my own, setting a pattern for my future relationships until I grew tired of heartbreak. All of our experiences impact the ways in which we show up today!

During the longest single period of my life, I decided to invest in multiple forms of therapy. At one point I was doing text therapy, talk therapy, and art therapy. I wanted nothing more than to break this pattern of staying silent about red flags and running from my problems. I needed to relearn how I translated my mother's advice, "You don't have to go back there" and turn the thought into one that encouraged me to tell the person why I was upset. Those reflections helped propel me toward my boldest self and healthier, more balanced relationships, but I can't say that journey didn't come with its fair share of casualties.

I admire people who are assertive and set boundaries. In my years of mastering boundary setting, I've also learned to honor and respect other people's feelings and time. As a result, I'm selective with whom I give my energy to, and in my growth, I've become even quicker to call out anyone who wrongs me. Instead of needing three, four, or five red flags to speak up, I'm able to prevent disappointment by letting go sooner and calling people out right away. I don't regret these decisions, but I often think about those people I've cut off, and I pray for them. I pray that they've since grown and that my decision doesn't haunt them or make them feel like a terrible person. In one instance I've taken the time to issue an apology, but for others, I've left it to God.

Do You Owe Someone an Apology?

Have you ever taken the time to think about whom you may owe an apology to? Would it help them process or move on if you did? Would it help you? Whether it concerns a minor oversight or a significant error, the act of apologizing can break a cycle that you never knew you were in the middle of. Perhaps you apologized in the past but never really meant it or fully understood why it was necessary, so you're considering returning to the conversation to share what you've processed since then. Sincere apologies serve as opportunities to mend rifts, allowing both the giver and the receiver of the apology to walk a path toward healing and understanding. It not only acknowledges the hurt caused but also signifies your willingness to take responsibility and make amends.

In my desire to end silence, with every subject touched and the close examination that I've taken with my elders, I wonder how many times my family has heard the words "I'm sorry," especially from those who mistreated or abused them. When I began this journey, I was perhaps in search of an apology for coming close to death in a way that could've been prevented, for the generational secrets, and for the silence that deprived me of chances to better understand myself. There was a time when I sought an apology from my father for his lack of verbal communication, and years when I didn't realize I also yearned for one from my mother. By unpacking my feelings in therapy, I learned that I didn't need an apology to forgive. What I was truly yearning for was understanding, the desire to know their whys and have conversation. I also wanted them to have the opportunity to know the impact of their decisions and the weight that I carried from my past with them. And so whether that was through a letter to my father or an uncomfortable phone call with my mother, I was able to get it out and accept that my effort was an apology to myself for walking alone with the pain.

The difficult conversations, confrontations, and discomfort are worth facing to understand parts of ourselves that are possibly unhealthy or uncover how we allowed ourselves to stay in unhealthy situations. To do the true preventative work that it takes to make the best decisions for our families, health, faith, career, and finances, we should know what factors play a role in where we land. We must learn who we are, and then understand why we are, to discover what we're capable of changing. We gain power in healthy confrontation, and history has shown us that remaining silent doesn't help any situation or issue get resolved. Looking back, I spent too many days quiet just to maintain the comfort of others, and there's a good chance several people still don't grasp the true effect of their actions on me, and maybe that's because in their version of the story, I'm not so innocent.

There's always room for improvement in how we treat others. As babies or small children, we are encouraged to apologize if we hurt another child's feelings or take away something that belongs to them. We might not mean it, and we may be upset that we have to do it, but our parents often make it a point to teach us that apologies can mend trust. Yet, the way in which it's being taught is questionable. While many would appreciate a prompt, genuine apology, insincere ones don't serve any helpful purpose. This is why a conversation about the impact of the child's behavior should take place before they issue the apology. In an article for *Time* magazine, social psychologist Cindy Frantz shared the following regarding the timing and effectiveness of an apology: "What we found is that there can be a temptation to offer an apology quickly. It's an effort to shut the whole incident down and move on. And that benefits the perpetrator, but it doesn't meet the needs of the victim . . . You can't deliver an effective apology until and unless the injured party believes that you fully understand what you did wrong. If the apology comes before that, it's not going to be seen as sincere."[3]

So what does a genuine apology look like, and when is the right time to give it? The best time to apologize is when you mean it.

- **IF YOU CAN'T UNDERSTAND WHY THE PERSON IS UPSET, ASK FOR CLARITY:** You can't apologize for something if you don't understand what went wrong and how your actions impacted the other party.

- **MAKE SURE YOU MEAN IT:** If your apology is sincere, you won't need immediate acceptance or a response that gives you comfort. Don't add pressure to the victim by expecting them to move on according to the timeline that works best for you.

- **EXPRESS WHAT YOU COULD HAVE DONE INSTEAD:** This shows that you not only feel bad but you understand how you could've handled the situation differently.

- **GIVE EXTRA CARE TO FAMILY AND FRIENDS:** With small, minor offenses it may be okay to send a text or email, but when a valued relationship is on the line, it's important that you give the apology more energy than you gave the offense.

- **ACKNOWLEDGE THAT THE BLAME BELONGS TO YOU AND ONLY YOU:** In his book *On Apology*, Aaron Lazare shares that it's important that the apology does not point the finger at the victim or put them at fault for the outcome. When apologizing by saying, "I'm sorry, but you got me so angry," it becomes less about accountability and more about making excuses.[4]

Why Do You Communicate the Way You Do?

Have you ever considered how your mental health and surrounding environment influence your preferred methods of communication or even the way you apologize? I grew up in a quiet house with a loud mind. My ADHD craved constant stimulation, and since I couldn't always verbally express my thoughts, I got creative with finding quiet ways to share. I embraced storytelling at a young age, from crafting magazines filled with articles and images to writing and designing my own books. I had journals for different topics, and there was a period through elementary and middle school, and perhaps even now, where I wrote more than I spoke.

Silent surroundings or environments where emotional expression is stifled can often inspire storytellers to find comfort in creating art. I've come to realize that I am a silent storyteller, using writing as my primary form of communication and self-expression. It enables me to release and sometimes refrain from using words I could possibly regret or I don't mean. While writing this book, my good friend Erica Dickerson, author of *Good Mom's Guide to Making Bad Choices*, suggested that I use voice notes to release my thoughts. She shared how easy the process of creating a book was for her because she could speak directly into her phone's notes app, using the voice dictation feature. The app would transcribe her words to text. This advice, although helpful for her and probably many others, left me stuck. The introverted, socially anxious me cringed at the thought of having to speak my ideas. Writing has always been my preferred mode above all others.

Looking back, I can explain my communication preferences based on my upbringing. Learning more about myself has always inspired me to examine if these traits I carry are mine alone or if they're generational. When I was a kid, my father would get upset with us over incomplete chores and write us letters to express his disappointment. He wrote them partly because he worked a lot and there was a chance we would come home when he wasn't there, but I believe he also wrote them because it was easier for him to express his frustrations that way. Sometimes my father would leave a letter on the kitchen counter, and we could feel his disappointment from the capital letters. I think I read them to myself in his yelling voice. Then he would come home and be in the best of moods. When my stepmother came along, she coincidentally had a similar approach to communication, which is probably why she and my father were so perfect for each other. She loved to write letters. When we would have disagreements or when she was disappointed by my actions, she would write me long letters and leave them for me to find in my room. This was her way of getting everything out and being heard, and maybe it was the only comfortable way she knew how to apologize. I appreciated the letters, and when I was ready, I would write back.

In the fields of psychology and communication studies, experts often discuss the four primary communication styles most humans possess: passive, aggressive, passive-aggressive, and assertive.

- **PASSIVE COMMUNICATORS** rarely seek attention and often avoid expressing their thoughts and feelings directly, prioritizing others' needs over their own. Passive parents might not openly express their needs or feelings, leading to a situation where their authority is undermined, and children may lack clear guidance or boundaries.

- **AGGRESSIVE COMMUNICATORS** often react before taking time to think through their decisions. They can be confrontational, blaming or attacking others, and disregard the feelings and needs of those around them. Aggressive parents often use stern or demanding tones, and may resort to yelling or punitive measures to enforce rules, sometimes without considering the child's feelings or perspective.

- **PASSIVE-AGGRESSIVE COMMUNICATORS** may appear passive to the outside world but act out their aggression covertly through sarcasm, backhanded compliments, or by avoiding conversations. Passive-aggressive parents might express dissatisfaction or disappointment through indirect means rather than addressing issues openly. They might use guilt-inducing comments, withdraw affection, or be inconsistently responsive to their children's needs as a form of control or punishment.

- **ASSERTIVE COMMUNICATORS** are often confident in their approach and use clear, honest, and respectful expressions of thoughts and feelings. Assertive parents communicate their expectations, rules, and feelings clearly and respectfully. They listen to their children's perspectives, validate their feelings, and engage in open dialogue to solve problems collaboratively.

What would you say is the communication style of the people who raised you? How does that match or bump against your own style? My father was both passive and aggressive, depending on the day. He either held things in completely or got upset when he was frustrated with my brother and me for carelessness or mess around the house. My mother was a gentle parent, but she was assertive and shared often. I never had to guess what she was thinking or what she needed.

What communication style would other people say you use the most? I encourage you to look at your childhood and see which specific moments influenced your behavior or informed why you have grown to communicate in this way. Dissecting how we speak and respond to people really matters and ultimately impacts what type of relationships we will have romantically and even with our children. While there's no right or wrong way to be a parent, our parents' words and delivery can impact everything from our self-esteem to how we resolve personal and professional issues as adults. This behavior is then easily transferred through the family for generations until someone is ready to unlearn the unhelpful habits.

Finding Forgiveness for Others

> "Never does the human soul appear so
> strong as when it forgoes revenge."
>
> —Edwin Hubbell Chapin

Some people will never apologize to us by choice or circumstance, but each day we have an opportunity to forgive. We have the choice to give grace and release ourselves of our grudges regardless of the person holding themselves accountable or being in denial. We are not responsible for their lack of awareness or lack of accountability, and we deserve forgiveness regardless of whether or not we hope to reconcile our differences with the person. You owe yourself more than anyone could ever give you.

Forgiving someone is not about releasing them of their wrongdoing. In fact, it's less about them and more about you. Professor of educational psychology and forgiveness expert Robert Enright said the following: "You can hang on to anger for a short time because it shows you're a person of worth and dignity, and no one should treat you this way. But then my question would be, if you hang on to that anger, what is it doing to you? Yes, it will empower you for a while. But characteristically over time, it brings us down with fatigue, rumination, becoming far more pessimistic in life."[5]

Research from the Stanford Forgiveness Projects shows that people who choose to forgive tend to embrace a more hopeful, optimistic outlook on life and become more compassionate.[6] Forgiveness can also improve our capacity to navigate conflicts more effectively. Additionally, numerous studies have shown that forgiving individuals often experience fewer physical stress symptoms, like back pain, muscle stiffness, dizziness, headaches, and stomach issues. Embracing forgiveness can not only elevate one's mental state but also boost their energy levels and general well-being. This is a hope I have for all of my family and future generations.

When a family member or friend passes away, or you're unable to communicate with them, it often doesn't give you a chance to choose a happy ending. Yet it's up to you to deal with the emotions, thoughts, and lingering feelings you might have when they pass. Give yourself grace and do the work to let go of the anger or pain. If at any point I feel like I'm unable to process on my own, I turn to my therapist or my faith. And when it comes to someone I've lost, I like to write them a letter, or talk to them out loud, imagining that they can hear me and that my words aren't wasted.

I come from a group of people who were severely traumatized and abused, and today the great-great-grandchildren of those abusers live among us. Some are our bosses, neighbors, or parents of our children's friends. African Americans could easily walk around with hate in their hearts for all of the many years of trauma and suffering we've experienced and carry, yet we've had to move on without apologies and put our energy toward a continued fight for justice and peace.

For centuries, there's been an argument around whether or not Black people deserve reparations. The idea, which promised freed slaves land as a form of reparations, was initially introduced immediately after the Civil War by General William Tecumseh Sherman in 1865. Yet the battle for acknowledgment and restitution was rejected until more recently, gaining momentum as part of a broader movement to address racial inequalities. The aim of reparations is layered. Its purpose is not to simply put money into the hands of those whose ancestors were enslaved and reduce the racial wealth gap, but many people see it as a long overdue apology for the centuries of systemic injustices that prevented African Americans from accessing wealth and homeownership opportunities from the beginning.

The modern reparations movement has gained significant support from various activists, organizations, and scholars. New York State assemblywoman Michaelle Solages has been vocal about the importance of addressing the legacies of slavery, emphasizing the need for healing within communities affected by generational trauma. "We want to make sure we are looking at slavery and its legacies," Solages stated, underlining the initiative as a step toward healing. "This is about beginning the process of healing our communities. There still is generational trauma that people are experiencing. This is just one step forward."[7] Although opposition exists, people who argue against reparations are often the same people who refuse to acknowledge the lasting legacy of slavery. Burying history and dismissing the African American experience, some see reparations as an issue that the current generation shouldn't have to address.

While we would love control over the outcome, reparations may never happen for the majority of Black Americans. The wrongs of many will never be admitted, and what happened in the past cannot be changed. The apologies we feel entitled to may not sound like the traditional expressions we're used to hearing, but we must accept this to find peace. We need to move forward and get free from these burdens.

Healer's Recap

- The point of looking back should be to move forward with great intention.

- The faster we move forward, the slower we feel, if ever.

- Even in situations where we need to cut ties or part ways with family and friends, we can do so in a way that allows for reflection, respect, and sharing before the relationship comes to an end.

- Through our childhood experiences, we learn how to engage with the outside world, and unknowingly, we can carry on our parents' communication styles with our children or relationships.

- Each day we have an opportunity to forgive. That doesn't mean it comes in the order of receiving an apology first. It also doesn't have to end with reconciliation after.

- You owe yourself more than anyone could ever give you.

- Forgiving someone is not about releasing them from their wrongdoing. In fact, it's less about them and more about you.

Chapter Ten

We Are Enough!

How much of an impact does external validation have in shaping your self-perception?

I have a beautiful obsession with studying the habits and minds of people who have persistently risen to the top of their careers or have taken leadership positions within their communities. I'm always intrigued by those who become the first, even if only within their families, and I often wonder how they had the courage to forge their own path. What did their self-talk look like? What was their formula? How did they come to believe that they were chosen or worthy?

It requires an admirable amount of confidence for any leader to step out into the world to build something big or create something new, to have the audacity to go against the grain. While all great leaders have vision, I know they also face roadblocks. So I find myself consistently studying and living between the pages of memoirs and biographies of those who persevered despite life's challenges. I find myself wanting to master this magical recipe of unshakeable self-belief.

Before becoming a mother to my son, becoming my sister Miracle's guardian was the most significant responsibility I had in someone else's life. And if there was one thing I've always prioritized in my role as her guardian and big sister, it was trying to build her self-confidence. The very first time I met her was at a funeral for a member of her family. Miracle was only four years old at the time, and I came to know her through my stepfather, who was also her great-uncle. I distinctly remember Miracle coming up to meet me. She was wearing a leopard dress and her hair was in unkempt braids, but despite the awkwardness I sensed in her, she was so sweet. Throughout our interaction, she kept her gaze lowered, only glancing up a few times to make brief eye contact. It was clear she found it challenging to connect, but the desire was there.

Shortly after we met, my mother and stepfather shared that Miracle's family was in the midst of some challenges, and, as a result, my mother and stepfather decided to keep her in their care. Miracle's mother had personal issues, which impacted her ability to care for all of her children. With four children in the home, Miracle's siblings were either facing foster care or living with their grandmother, who had health issues to prioritize. Empathizing with their situation, my mother promptly assumed guardianship of Miracle from the time she was four until she was about ten years old. As Miracle grew older, her relationship with her family was limited to telephone calls, until her biological mother expressed a desire for her to return home. Initially, I was hesitant about Miracle moving back with her mother. Given her circumstances, I felt as though the best living arrangement for her was with my mom. Regardless of where she resided, I promised Miracle that I would continue to be in her life as a big sister, and it was a promise I was determined to keep. Thankfully her biological family was open to this and respected our bond.

Every other weekend, I would pick Miracle up from her mother's to take her back to my home. Over the years, we even made it a point to spend holidays and summer breaks together. When she could, she called outside of those moments for me to come get her any chance I could. Gradually, she became reliant on me for her most basic needs, and I was always more than happy to offer support. I loved the time I spent with Miracle. She was the sweetest, funniest kid, and most of all, I loved the role I played in her life, stepping in not just for her family but for my mother who had moved down to Florida, miles away.

Helping raise Miracle from someone else's home had its challenges. On two occasions she traveled to my home with bed bugs, causing me to have to get my entire apartment fumigated. If you've ever dealt with those disgusting sleep critters, then you know you have to take extreme measures to get rid of them as soon as possible. On both occasions, I was forced to wash every piece of clothing I owned, wrap everything in trash bags, flip the furniture, and temporarily stay in a hotel while my place was uninhabitable for two weeks. This took a toll on me financially, yet the most upsetting part was knowing she was living among the bugs.

The bed bugs weren't the only issues she faced at home. At age fifteen, Miracle's biological mother passed away. With her passing, she left her children to the care of Miracle's grandmother. A year after her mother's passing, Miracle's grandmother passed from COVID. Miracle and her siblings were blindsided and heartbroken by these losses.

When I met my husband that same year, on our very first date, I mentioned the possibility that I may one day need to become the guardian of a teenage girl. And I was right. About a year and half later, Miracle ended up moving into my one-bedroom apartment, where my husband had recently moved in.

With Miracle moving into our home, I knew I needed to set some ground rules. I also knew the importance of providing her with structure and offering her an environment that was supportive of her education and needs. We established a bedtime, created rules about her phone use, and together we worked toward a new beginning in a place we both felt confident she would be able to call home until she was ready to go out on her own. I showed that through my actions, and I made it especially clear with my words. This would be her last stop as a child.

To this day, we have an exceptional relationship. She's both my little sister and my best friend. For years, I treaded the tightrope between being a fun and disciplinarian figure in her life. Having cultivated a relationship of trust, Miracle paid little attention to others' instructions but always heeded and respected mine. Navigating this journey without any maternal experience was challenging, but I imparted the values my parents instilled in me, guiding her toward her own path, and I made sure we constantly talked about how she was experiencing things around her and areas where I could be of assistance. We leaned into respectful dialogue, and even in the moments when I felt frustrated or disappointed, I communicated in a way that was neither belittling nor harsh. It was crucial to demonstrate to Miracle that conflict and discipline could be managed respectfully. Yet, as she embarks on her college journey, and even as I step into my next chapter of raising another child, I find myself wondering if I did enough.

Miracle is breaking generational cycles, and I couldn't be prouder. While raising her, I wanted her to know that she had options to pursue all of her dreams. I wanted her to know her worth is not impacted by her circumstances. With this in mind, communication has been a continuous effort for Miracle and me. There have been times when I would literally beg her to speak or share the things going on in that brain of hers. In the past, her preference was always to keep her thoughts to herself, even if it pained her to do so. For years her feelings were often neglected, and I believe she chose to shut down as a way to protect herself. As the youngest in her family, she was often told what to do, and as a young girl surrounded by brothers, her emotions were frequently downplayed.

It took nearly eighteen years for Miracle to finally start opening up without being prompted. Lately, her text responses have evolved from no response at all or one-word replies to complete sentences. Today Miracle attends college, works part-time, and maintains excellent grades. Even when she's living on campus, I sleep well at night knowing that she's safe and has a clean place to rest her head. She checks in and we speak almost every day.

Recently, I texted her and asked if I could ask her a few personal questions. I wanted to learn about her struggles with confidence, if any. I told her we could go over them on FaceTime or in whatever way she felt most comfortable. Surprisingly, she replied, "Let's text." I think she was excited about my random request for an interview and couldn't wait until she was in a quiet place to engage. It was unlike our daily interactions for me to ask permission to ask questions, but I've found that mentally preparing people for deep or personal questions can be helpful. It also helps me discern when it's "a good time" to talk.

To start, I asked her a question I've never asked her before: "As a child, what were you insecure about?" She quickly started typing. "As a child I was insecure about my home environment. When I moved back to Brooklyn to live with my biological family, I felt like I didn't have what all the other kids had, and I thought they would think less of me since I didn't have a nice home and two parents and the new clothes."

I fired off my second question before responding to the first by asking, "Growing up, who affirmed you and made you feel confident?" Expecting her to say my mother or perhaps one of her teachers, her response was a beautiful surprise. "You made me feel confident because you always pushed me to do better, even if I didn't believe in myself. You showed me anything is possible as long as you work for it, and I got to see it firsthand from you, so I knew I could do anything as long as I have your support."

Thinking back, I never focused on Miracle's physical appearance when affirming her. I often told her she was smart, capable, and caring. I aimed to instill in her a kind of confidence that would help her navigate life and hold onto her dreams. Today, Miracle will be the first of a total of fourteen siblings from her mother and father to graduate from college. While I was supporting her and affirming her as a child, I wanted nothing more than for her to grow up to know that she could build the life she's always wanted, as long as she believed in herself and chased after her dreams. To hear her share that I gave her confidence might've been one of the biggest compliments I've ever received, and it meant that, in those moments where I questioned if I'd done enough, I had.

Having supportive figures during formative years can significantly impact an individual's self-esteem and future leadership capabilities, helping them to break cycles. When I think about my own childhood, I remember my mother affirming my dreams, a degree of support she never experienced from her own mother. As humans we all yearn to have a support system even if it's only one person. Having someone to validate your beliefs and ideas can have a deeply positive effect.

I believe that advancing beyond generations of feeling inadequate or unworthy also requires significant positive self-talk or affirmations, which are present-tense statements used to positively influence one's thoughts and build confidence. They can help you reject negative or self-deprecating thoughts and allow you to refocus on the possible positive outcomes of your current situation. Affirmations help us break free from self-imposed limiting beliefs. By repeating these empowering statements, we challenge the negative narratives that often constrain us.

Have you ever been so close to quitting or walking away from a challenge, only to tell yourself "I can do this" or "I'm almost there"? It's this kind of self-coaching that goes the longest way in affirming our behaviors. It's a "Yes, I can" attitude and a "I can do that" mindset that help us unlock new potential and break generational barriers. These statements are so powerful, yet they don't need to be spoken aloud. When I recite affirmations, they are usually in my mind. I can be in a room full of people and coach myself through an insecurity without anyone ever knowing. My friend Angie, a leading C-suite financial professional, practices her affirmations at the start of her day in the shower. Whatever method works best for you is what you should lean into.

My adult journey of positive self-talk was necessary to avoid descending into a negative mental space. When the doctors first gave me my thoracic endometriosis diagnosis and informed me that I would have to live on birth control or remove my uterus, eliminating the option to ever bear children, I made an effort to maintain a positive outlook. And when the universe continued to send me repeated lessons and men with broken wings, I kept telling myself or perhaps God, "I know there is a good man out there for me. I will find someone to love me like I love others."

Statements starting with "I am," "I will," or "I can" are deeply rooted in the struggles and resilience of oppressed people around the world, and they keep even the most depressed or saddened people from settling or believing they deserve less. When you believe your words, you give them power. My willingness to affirm myself helped me find the patience to receive my biggest blessings. Affirm with me as we do this work together: I will be the catalyst for positive transformation in my family.

Overcoming Microaggressions and Generational Unworthiness

Reflecting on the dehumanizing experience of slavery in America, you will find that affirmations helped to preserve ideas, identities, and aspirations. These verbal or internal expressions served as subtle vehicles for conveying hope and encouraged resistance. By reclaiming and vocalizing these forms of expression, enslaved people engaged in an early form of decolonization and created Negro spirituals, subtly undermining the oppressive narratives imposed on them while creating a stronger sense of shared identity and strength. When I close my eyes, I can still hear my grandmother singing one particular Negro spiritual: "Lord, I know I've been changed. I said that I know I've been changed. I know I've been changed; angels in Heaven done signed my name." This was a song that was passed down through generations so Black Americans could continue to assert their humanity, their aspirations for freedom, and their faith in arriving at a positive outcome when life ends.

Moving forward through history, the legacy of using one's voice to affirm one's humanity became a cornerstone in the fight for African American freedoms and civil rights. Influential figures like Maya Angelou, Toni Morrison, Audre Lorde, and James Baldwin harnessed the power of words to uplift, inspire, and assert the beauty, dignity, and resilience of Black identity. The evolution of modern-day affirmations has become a self-help practice for all races. Today, influencers like licensed counselor Faith Broussard and authors Alex Elle and Lalah Delia use their platforms to empower their communities in the midst of whatever they may be facing, giving support to those who may not have another place or person to turn to for similar messages of hope.

Affirming ourselves, our families, and our children is a critical act of generational care. When we affirm ourselves, but especially our children, we do the following:

- Enhance their self-esteem

- Empower them to follow through on their big ideas

- Support their emotional and mental well-being

- Promote positive behavior and outcomes

- Spark an optimistic attitude

- Build resilience

At the heart of professor Geoffrey Cohen's teachings, he champions the concept of self-affirmations as a way to "make the self firm." As a Stanford University professor of psychology, he believes that children can build an unshakable sense of self when they connect deeply with their core values.[1] It is this way of thinking that I wish to give to all of my family members. A key figure in the abolitionist movement and famous author Frederick Douglass once said, "It is easier to build strong children than to repair broken men." While I agree with this statement, we should not be discouraged in wanting to help our elders and adult family members. In this journey, I've seen change in my grandfather, who now has the opportunity to learn how to read along with his great-grandchild, and I see this in the improvements my father and I have made in communicating with one another. Our elders can heal. It will just take work.

Everyone deserves to set themselves free from the shackles of craving acceptance or approval from others or believing the false narratives that were taught during childhood. In my adult life, I've started the practice of offering myself spontaneous affirmations that I may not need today but will most likely need in the future. I write out the affirmations on a small slip of paper and then hide them within pages of books that I know I will eventually read. I leave them in my bathroom and at the bottom of my dresser drawers. Sometimes I stick them in the most unexpected places, knowing that sometimes a simple affirmation can redirect my day or mindset and help me stay on track with the things I desire to claim over my life. A simple affirmation can improve my emotional well-being.

My Go-To Affirmations

- I release myself from the desire to be accepted.

- I live in my authenticity, and I'm loved because of it.

- I reject conformity.

- My spirit is kind.

- My dreams are waiting for me to arrive.

- I'm not my past mistakes. I am evolving for my assignment.

- I am wealthy in the mind and in the spirit.

Building on the foundation my mother laid for me, the affirmations I live by today act as reinforcements, fortifying my mental and emotional defenses. My affirmations are constantly changing, evolving with me as I grow. They keep me well and serve as personal reminders, emphasizing that I am capable of overcoming obstacles and breaking cycles of doubt and self-criticism that, if left unchecked, can hinder my progress. They help me see myself as worthy, countering everything that my ancestors were told they were not.

I believe that the love I experience today is the result of affirmations I have consciously cultivated over time. On our wedding save-the-dates, Kelsei and I sent out refrigerator magnets of an affirmation that I wrote out as the theme for our wedding with the hashtag #ForeverWell. The affirmation:

"A Union Manifested:

I am well alone. I am well with you.

Together we are healthy. Together we are love."

I hoped to inspire others with our request. I wanted people to see the affirmation each day and perhaps manifest healthy love in their lives as well.

To inspire Miracle, my family, and even my friends, I've learned to not only use positive self-talk but to model the behavior of someone who believes wholeheartedly in the goodness of the world. This same behavior is being modeled for me by the people I choose to surround myself with. In the outside world, I have a long list of community leaders, phenomenal mothers, and friends that I look to for inspiration. Our affirmations are backed by actions. What starts with an idea or repeated statement becomes a challenge that we work to live out in real life. By doing this, I show myself and the world that if I say I'm going to do something, I will follow through, and if I believe it, I'm going to show you that I am it.

Questions for Yourself

Knowing yourself well is key to filtering through the voices and values you wish to prioritize. Take a moment to answer the following questions:

- When I talk to myself, whose voice do I hear? Is it my own or the voice of those who raised me?

- How would I describe my inner voice?

- What differences do I hear in how I encourage myself versus how my elders encouraged me?

The next step is understanding why you speak to yourself in the way you do. Even for me, I meditate on my affirmations and ask myself why I need to hear these particular messages. I think about what experiences left me desiring these words and what actions I need to take to turn these affirmations into practices. Prior to meeting Kelsei, an exercise that I practiced was spending time in the morning affirming myself with positive self-talk. I was working to build my best self so when my husband did come along, he would get the best version of me. I would start my day having these moments of pause with myself, whether it was with a toothbrush in my mouth, after I washed my face, or before I dressed for the day. It's still something I do, paying attention each day to what I'm telling myself.

If you had a hard time answering the questions above, set a timer for two minutes, stand in front of the mirror, and simply look at yourself until the time is up. Observe your physical body and the thoughts that flood your mind. When you're finished, write down everything you thought to yourself. If you need prompts or questions to inspire your writing, ask yourself the following:

- Was I present with myself today?

- Did my thoughts center around what I was seeing or feeling?

- Were the thoughts of myself positive or negative? Why?

- Am I kinder to myself or others?

Affirming myself has led me to every beautiful gift in my life. It's saved me from repeating cycles of unhappiness and unfulfillment that so many of my family members have experienced. It has brought me closer to myself as well as my faith, and it has helped me build up others, including the children in my life.

Affirming Your Loved Ones

Be aware of your words and how they may stick with people. Recently, I've adopted a new habit of giving my family members empowering compliments every time we interact with each other, sharing something that could propel them toward decisions that help them shine in their unique light and feel more confident about themselves. It could be as simple as, "Talking to you always puts me at ease," "I'm proud of . . ." or "You bring so much laughter to everyone around you." I watch as these expressions, which are seemingly small, put a smile on the faces of the ones I love.

Do you offer others encouragement? Do you celebrate the strengths of your loved ones? With your words, you have the power to spark the dreams or behaviors that build future leaders, not just in the world but within your community and in your home. Be mindful of how you can speak love, success, and hope within your circle. Know that there's no greater feeling than helping someone break cycles that don't support their highest potential. I challenge you to encourage three people today!

Healer's Recap

- Broken confidence can be repaired.

- Positive self-talk will save you!

- People will tell you that you are not enough; this is a lie.

- Advancing beyond generations of inadequacy or unworthiness requires significant confidence, self-belief, and self-efficacy.

- Positive affirmations can provide the boost of confidence and reassurance you need to tackle your greatest challenges.

- Be mindful of your self-talk and how it was formed. Is your idea of self formed through the ideas and opinions of others?

- Not only do you have the power to build the life you want, but you also have the power to help someone else do the same.

Chapter Eleven

Advocate for a Better World

Is there a social issue that's triggering for you or your family? Do your beliefs derive from what's been passed down to you, or have you formed an opinion through your own earth-side experience?

In America, if you're Black, you're three times more likely to be killed during a police encounter.[1] Over 50 percent of the homeless population spent time in the foster care system.[2] Forty-two percent of youth in the juvenile justice system are Black, even though African Americans compromise only 15 percent of youth in the nation.[3] With this data, my contributions to social impact almost feel obligatory, rather than a choice. And as a Black woman, I believe that people should always advocate for what's fair and just, to improve the world we live in and to reduce the harm and stress within the community.

What portraits or reminders proudly hang on the walls of your family homes? I've always been intentional about the messages I surround myself with, whether online, in the company I keep, or in my home. There's a picture that adorns the wall of my home office, subtly making itself known in the background of my virtual meetings. It's a print by the artist Sumuyya Khader that boldly displays the phrase "Stand Up, Speak Out" in thick black letters. The black-and-white piece draws inspiration from the social justice movements of 2020, emphasizing the importance of raising one's voice. What obviously drew me to the piece was the artist's ability to convey the timely reminder that we can no longer remain passive observers in the fight against oppression.

On the opposite wall, however, hangs a massive piece by Kevin "Wak" Williams called *2020: Civil Unrest*, also inspired by 2020. It depicts a young girl at a protest, holding a sign made from the remnants of a cardboard box that reads, "No justice, no peace." Ironically, both pieces are within close proximity of each other and can be found unintentionally anchored by additional artwork depicting Black women, displaying side-eyes and pursed lips.

I've never given much thought as to why these artworks resonate with me until now. When I chose to invest in these particulars pieces, I thought about the experience of my visitors—guests who would spend time in my home and get curious about the artwork. I thought about how it would make them feel and if it would inspire curiosity or conversation. Collectively, these pieces serve as a visual narrative that speaks to my experience. There's just something about the side-eye expressions of the women on my walls that reminds me of individuals, like them and like me, who are fighting on the front lines and looking to others for acknowledgment and support. Whenever I'm present enough to soak in my surroundings, I look at these pieces and feel inspired to make a difference by actively participating in movements and campaigns that improve living conditions for my community and the youth I serve. With these pieces over my shoulders, I'm reminded to "speak out."

I've always felt compelled to use my voice for the voiceless, even if it ruffles a few feathers. As a child, I wouldn't say I was a tattletale, but I would step in to correct someone's actions if they went against the rules. That didn't make me popular, but it sure made me proud. In my mind, my behavior was warranted because I truly cared about order and fairness, and it was difficult for me to sit back and watch people take advantage of situations or mistreat people.

Growing up, I was the antithesis of my brother, who was shy, reserved, and reclusive. Despite being four years older, he often turned to me, his little sister, to request things from our parents on his behalf.

Interestingly, my brother's ten-year-old son carries many of his traits. He also turns to his younger sister, asking her to involve herself and request things from the adults. Partly shy and perhaps timid, my nephew encourages my niece to take charge. Without fear, she asks for what they want, whether it's candy or a sleepover at Titi Coley's house. Were you the kid who spoke up and asked for what you wanted, or did you tend to take what was given to you?

When you grow up practicing how to ask for what you want, you get better at advocating for yourself and others. My father was a great parent, but he was also a strict disciplinarian. I was just as afraid of him as my brother was, but I was never too afraid to ask for what I needed. When my father disagreed with one of my requests, I would often move on quickly, seldom succumbing to disappointment. Dealing with feelings of disappointment was a skill I was forced to acquire early on. His sharp "no" or "Cole, don't bother me right now" made it easier for me to process rejection in my adult life. Speaking up as a child allowed me to foster courage and build the confidence required to ask for what I needed, without the fear of rejection. I've come to realize that I've adopted a "the worst they can say is no" attitude with most things.

Good Trouble

Looking back on the lives of the women who came before me, I'm reminded of my strength and innate ability to model healthy habits to inspire the next generation. I know that while I seek better approaches to the world around me, I can make the biggest difference at home with my family. At home, just like in the world, there's no guarantee that my voice will be respected, but I know that at the minimum it will be heard.

The first wave of courageous feminists risked it all to use their voices. African American women, in particular, played a pivotal role in shaping movements for justice and equality in the early nineteenth century by standing at the forefront of abolitionism. They knew that mere participation wasn't enough to create change, volunteering to establish organizations and initiatives that addressed racial and gender injustices. Among these trailblazers was Maria Stewart, who is known for being one of the first and most courageous women in the United States to speak publicly on political issues, despite her race.

Maria Stewart shared her first groundbreaking public lecture in Boston, Massachusetts, in the early 1830s, marking a pivotal moment for women, particularly African American women, in the public sphere. Faced with a mix of admiration and backlash, Stewart's actions reflected the deeply rooted racial and gender prejudices of her time. Yet, her oratory and written work vigorously challenged these injustices, advocating for equal education, gender equality, and equitable economic opportunities for the African American community. Oh to be in that audience that day. While the specific content of that first lecture is not widely cited, her subsequent speeches and published works underscore her fight for freedom, education, and equality. In her essays and speeches, Stewart challenged her audiences with provocative questions and statements, such as:

- "Are we not as capable of learning as white people are?"

- "It is not the color of the skin that makes the man or the woman, but the principle formed in the soul."

- "You can but die, if you make the attempt; we shall certainly die if you do not."

- "All the nations of the earth are crying out for liberty and equality. Away away with tyranny and oppression."

She lit a fire within those who were growing tired of being seen as less than human, less than equal. Stewart's advocacy was revolutionary not only for its direct challenge to the societal norms of her time but also for laying the foundation for future generations of feminists and civil rights activists who would follow in her footsteps. Her work and words remain an inspiration to this day.

Another widely recognized figure is the first female African American preacher in the United States, Jarena Lee. In breaking significant religious and societal boundaries by preaching about faith and freedom, her journey was far from narrow. Around 1807, while living in Philadelphia, Lee believed she was called by God to dedicate her life to being a preacher. This was troubling for most to understand at the time because women were not allowed to speak up in church. These restrictions were based on the Bible scripture, "Let your women keep silence in the churches: for it is not permitted unto them to speak."[4] When Lee asked the bishop at her church if she could preach, her request was denied. Disappointed but not discouraged, she penned the bishop a letter: "If the man may preach because the Savior died for him, why not the woman? Seeing he died for her also. Is he not a whole Savior instead of a half one?"[5]

Lee eventually moved to New Jersey in 1811, marrying Pastor Jason Lee and giving birth to six children. Even in her roles as a mother and wife, she couldn't shake off the feeling that she was meant to preach, but even her husband wasn't on board. Every man she looked to, including her husband, wanted to suppress her voice. When her husband passed away in 1817, Jarena went back to Philadelphia and returned to her former church, feeling more convinced than ever that she was supposed to preach. Then, in 1819, during a church service, the guest preacher got so nervous he couldn't speak. Jarena stood up and took over, finishing the sermon for him. The bishop, Richard Allen, who initially told her no, was so impressed with her ministry that he changed his mind and let her become the first female minister of the African Methodist Episcopal (AME) Church. An unstoppable force, Lee saw that as the beginning of her purpose and began traveling to preach to anyone who would listen. As a Black woman, I owe my life and liberties not only to my ancestors but to women like Maria Stewart and Jarena Lee, and I pray their names are never forgotten.

"When the whole world is silent, even
one voice becomes powerful."
—**Malala Yousafzai**

In 2012, Malala Yousafzai, a fifteen-year-old Pakistani teenager, was shot in the head by a Pakistani Taliban gunman while making her way home from school. The horrific attack caught the world's attention, highlighting the ongoing struggles faced by women and girls in Pakistan and the Taliban's constant threats to girls' education. Despite being targeted for her outspoken advocacy for girls' education, Malala spoke up and used her voice to fight back. She emerged as one of the most powerful voices and a champion in the fight for education and equality. Because of her heroic efforts, she went on to speak at the United Nations, met with leaders worldwide, co-authored a book titled *I Am Malala: The Girl Who Stood Up for Education and Was Shot by the Taliban*, and cofounded the Malala Fund to support educational initiatives for girls in underprivileged areas.

To this day, women continue to risk their lives for their fundamental rights and basic freedoms. And in America where respect for women is selective, domestic violence is one of the leading causes for homelessness among women and children. As beneficiaries of women's sacrifices, we must defend and protect all women. If there was ever an uncertainty of a social issue that you could get behind, you could always stand in solidarity with women, especially the women in your family. We need more allies and less gender bias.

There are countless opportunities for us to carry the legacy of those who came before us into the future. If you've ever felt powerless or unsure of where to begin, here are some actions you can undertake to begin using your voice for good:

- Find a social cause that you're passionate about and do your research to fully understand where the challenges lie. Take the time to research political figures, organizers, or leaders who are already doing the work and inquire how you can get behind them.

- Uplift the voices of others. We all play a crucial role in the movement as long as we're working together to further the agenda. Attend events, fundraisers, protests, and rallies to support organizers and people on the frontlines.

- Don't focus on the likes and dislikes. History has a Rolodex of important leaders who have all had enemies and skeptics, and they still made a major social impact. Do your research when you come across information or online advocacy posts, and share the ones that are accurate to spread awareness. Post educational information that matters to you.

- Consider pursuing a career path that creates a positive impact.

- Join a nonprofit organization board, church, or volunteer group, or create a department within your organization that allows you to use not only your voice but your gifts and talents for the benefit of others. These roles will not only make you feel fulfilled, they will allow you to contribute to your community and support causes you care about.

- Vote if you're able. Your voice matters, and voting allows you to contribute to decisions that affect education, health care, infrastructure, and more. It offers an opportunity for representation that we should not take for granted.

Generational Impact of Speaking Up

Advocacy is not defined by the volume of your voice, but rather the actions behind your words. This effort can start right at home if you choose to break the cycle of silence that might have been passed down through generations. It's in the group chats you share with your siblings and cousins to talk about important family matters, or it's in the family gatherings or meetings to discuss ways you can support each other when in need. It's in the work you're doing now to inspire healthy dialogue within your family.

Starting to break the silence within your family can be as straight-forward as standing up for a family member who is suffering due to outdated or harmful generational mindsets and traditions. Many times, these long-standing beliefs can have negative mental or even physical implications on our family members. By speaking up for your family members, you initiate conversations that challenge the status quo and invite people to reevaluate or even question their beliefs.

I remember sitting in the living room with my aunt and my younger cousin Renee, who expressed to her mother that she was grappling with depression. Without missing a beat, her mother's response was, "You're not depressed." Her mother was quick to dis-miss Renee's truth and reject her cry for help. Having grown up around depression, I understand that it's not something people typ-ically broadcast. Being in the room with someone openly discussing it, I recognized the moment as an opportunity to lean in and offer support. The last thing someone needs when they're facing mental health issues is to feel invalidated or alone.

Respectfully, I chimed in and said, "If she's saying she's depressed, she might be." This annoyed her mother even more, who responded by bringing up irrelevant information. Trying to convince her daugh-ter that she was not depressed, my aunt went through a list of things Renee should be doing to feel well. My aunt didn't realize at the time how harmful her response was, but we later talked about it when my cousin wasn't around. She needed to be removed from the situation to process her daughter's revelation and her response, and when she was ready, she was able to approach the topic more gently. There's nothing wrong with feeling depressed, and no one should be made to feel bad about it. If anything, the people closest to you should support you in finding the right resources to help you navigate it.

I recognized this generational cycle instantly, having seen similar reactions from my own parents to things they didn't understand. Both of my grandmothers had to raise children on their own, often with limited patience, so they lacked education on confronting trauma and the effects of dismissing or silencing a child's feelings when it seemed inconvenient to engage. This pattern of behavior, possibly even harsher in their own experiences, is unfortunately common in many households, a reflection of the coping mechanisms and responses we've been taught and how we've been treated by others. In many cases, it's often chalked up to "tough love."

Part of my resistance to repeating unhealthy generational cycles is advocating to normalize conversations about mental health. I've already begun this journey in my work advocating for neurodivergent children. Many parents today were not afforded the opportunity to be diagnosed in their childhoods, which could have helped them better understand their unique brain functioning. In doing so, they would have been able to come to terms with conditions like ADHD, Autism Spectrum Disorder, Oppositional Defiant Disorder, anxiety, or depression and go on to lead a healthy life with a clear understanding that there was nothing innately wrong with them. Now, these parents are taking a stand, advocating in schools and speaking up for their children in hopes of providing them with a better opportunity to learn and feel supported in the ways they deserve.

It's so important to raise children to be advocates, not only for themselves but also those around them. This is how we build a more empathetic world. For generations within my family, it was known as the ultimate disrespect if a child "talked back" to elders. My cousins and I weren't raised to reject any rules or question authority. We were told that doing so made us bad children. Yet, raising Miracle has shown me how ignorant it is to expect to mold a child into neurotypical thinking and familial patterns that are outdated or even inflexible. Here are some questions you can ask to inspire your children to use their voice:

- Did you see or hear something that you disagreed with today? How did that make you feel? How did you respond?

- Do you understand why we have house rules? Do you understand why rules also exist in your classroom?

- Are there any boundaries you wish other people would respect in order to make you feel more comfortable?

  - For younger children, you might choose to simplify this a bit by asking them if there is anything they wish people wouldn't do so they'd feel more comfortable.

- Do you have any questions for me, or is there anything you're curious about?

Asking these questions will help them not only better understand themselves but also improve their understanding of the people around them, especially those in positions of authority. Since children are naturally curious and inclined to ask questions, why not encourage them to ask the kind of questions that lead to a deeper understanding of how the world works? This way, they can learn how to make their own contributions to it.

Sometimes, the generational impact of speaking up can be the thing to help your family detach future generations from dire, unhealthy practices and conditions. Environmental justice is a sweeping global issue that is directly impacting those most vulnerable. It's not merely about saving trees and wildlife; environmental justice strives to ensure every person, no matter their background, receives an equitable future. We must acknowledge that we are all interconnected and that one person's actions, thoughts, and behaviors can and will inevitably impact those around them. Today, environmental justice advocates of all ages are speaking up to save their families, creating a ripple effect throughout their communities.

Inspired by his mother's activism, Xiuhtezcatl Martinez chose to join the movement by using his voice at the tender age of six. As an Indigenous environmental activist and the youth director of Earth Guardians, Xiuhtezcatl dove into the climate justice movement motivated by his deep connection to his Indigenous roots and a strong belief in the importance of protecting the Earth for future generations.

Throughout his career, he has taken the stage at the United Nations multiple times and has engaged in significant legal confrontations with the US government, holding them accountable for failing to protect the environment for those who will inherit it. Today, Xiuhtezcatl is still fiercely advocating for the planet.

Questions for Yourself

- Who relies on my voice, and do I use it enough? Are there any family members or community members who may need me to speak on their behalf now or in the future? Do I feel prepared to advocate on their behalf?

- Am I afraid to use my voice in certain spaces or around certain people? Why?

- How often do I hold my thoughts to myself? Is this for the best or is this causing myself or anyone around me harm?

Your voice is your most valuable possession. And as my husband, Kelsei, who is the head of social impact for a major company, would say, "Think of your voice as a key. It can unlock many doors; it can also shut others. Be mindful of how you use it and thoughtful about what you unlock with it. As you speak boldly, recognize that not everyone' might like it or agree. That's okay. What's amazing is that your voice is a unique tool that can make a difference in your community today and in the lives of generations of people to come."

There's a massive range of global and localized issues we can get behind. Even as I write this, new social issues are emerging in response to evolving societal norms, technological advancements, and global events. We must "speak up and speak out" if we care in the slightest or if we feel the barest sense of gratitude for the ancestors who fought before us. After all, I believe that's part of our purpose here on earth.

Healer's Recap

- Never forget to "stand up, speak out" for yourself and others.

- Great risks are needed for big changes.

- Advocacy is not defined by the volume of your voice, but rather the actions behind your words.

- Empower children to be their best advocates. Never discourage them from asking for what they want.

- Your voice is a key. Use it to open doors as needed.

- Never be selective in your respect for women. Support and protect all women.

- New social issues are emerging in response to evolving societal norms, technological advancements, and global events. Find the ones that speak to you and get behind them with pride.

Chapter Twelve

Joy Out Loud

How often do you celebrate yourself?

Doing the work can feel exhausting—the salaried work, the family work, the self-work, and especially the healing work. The chosen few, like you and I, who desire more for ourselves and our families, can find ourselves carrying the heaviest burdens, seemingly contributing more mind power to each day and its arising challenges. Examining our ancestry and understanding how our families have contributed to both our joy and hardships can lead to overwhelming emotions. Yet, the generational cycle breakers—although totally consumed with their daily schedules—still find time to dive into books, listen to podcasts, and pursue supplementary information online or at events in a continuous effort to evolve. While it seems commendable, it can negatively impact our mental and physical health if we're not careful.

Doing the work—for family or for community—though noble, can simultaneously take a toll and lead to burnout. In our efforts, we might find ourselves taking on tasks to help others or passion projects that force us to work longer hours and sacrifice our sleep and boundaries. When we're not practicing self-care, acts of kindness can leave us feeling depleted. Then with the little time we have, we might find ourselves consumed by news, entertainment television, and social media, often leaving us struggling to dedicate time to what's in front of us or rest. Yet, in knowing we can improve our lives in so many areas, we still end up sacrificing parts of ourselves and making excuses for our lack of time.

The exhaustion we face on our journey to break cycles may come in waves, but it has helped me understand why so many generations have opted for silence; if we're honest about how we're really feeling, the obvious solution would be change. I knew an organizer who always carried such low energy. He did amazing work in the world, uplifting spirits and bringing joy to others, but whenever I was around him, I felt a sense of sadness. He seemed to switch on an alter ego, transforming himself when it came time to rally support, but away from the spotlight he retreated into a shell. When he wasn't speaking at a protest or standing on a stage, his tone of voice would change. Speaking slowly, with a voice tinged with weariness, he slogged his way through most conversations. Those who knew him closely could sense the immense weight upon him that suggested he was either overwhelmed by the work or simply unhappy. I could understand him. It is common to meet people with a similar disposition in the work we do.

The other day I sat in a room full of city officials, celebrating the opening of my foundation's first free mental wellness store for kids in NYC's foster care system. It was single-handedly one of the biggest moments in my career, yet as I sat there, listening to the commissioner's praise, my mind shifted to that organizer and how he probably felt on a regular basis. Although the moment was one to celebrate my achievements, for a quick minute, I let in the weight of all the things that hadn't been done and began to think about the suffering of the children in other states. It was not the time or place to venture into such a dark place, but I was there, nonetheless, and it was probably visible all over my face. A wave of guilt washed over me as we sat there in our best business attire, patting ourselves on the back for work we were supposed to be doing in the first place. But the longer I was in that room, the more I began to drown in my own negativity, robbing myself of a moment I had worked so hard to create.

Looking around the room, I made eye contact with one of my board members, who probably recognized the shift in my energy. Sitting in the front row, they stared back at me with the biggest, warmest smiles. Snapping out of my haze, I returned their smiles. Though it was such a simple gesture, it allowed me to lock back in on the speaker at the podium. The reality was, we had done fantastic work creating a wellness store that took years of planning. Why would I deprive myself of the joy I deserved in celebrating the progress I'd made because of the overwhelming thoughts of needing to do more?

Some of us are persistently haunted by the idea that our work isn't complete until everything has been tackled, but the issue with this is that our to-do list is never-ending. And our ability to focus on the undone can keep us in a state of unfulfillment, even during some of our biggest life moments. Over the years, I've had to learn to pay attention to the thoughts that flow through my mind, especially during moments when I'm in the company of others. It's almost as if my brain has to act as a filter, removing contaminants and impurities to keep my thoughts clear and focused on what's in front of me. As a person living with ADHD, my thoughts often wander into what needs to be done or future planning around big ideas. I've had to learn how to refocus my drifting contemplations on the present moment or the good in order to maintain my mental health and allow myself to experience happiness, regardless of what's happening at home or at work.

Are you taking advantage of moments that allow for you to create happy memories with family members or yourself? Sometimes we need to check ourselves and ask if this present situation is a "joy moment." We must ask ourselves if we're fully present, embracing our surroundings and celebrating ourselves. We all need and deserve joy. Look back at how hard our elders worked. Look back at the restrictions placed on your elders to be free to embrace fun. During slavery, my ancestors faced strict restrictions on their leisure activities. Any form of enjoyment, including the pursuit of joy or unauthorized community gatherings, was perceived as an act of disobedience.

Can you imagine not having the privilege to relax on your couch or take a nap when you're lacking rest? For my ancestors, rest could lead to severe punishment, even death. With an intimate understanding of this, I am always left with a sense of guilt, knowing that I should live in more gratitude and appreciation for the option to wake up each day and move around the world in the way I need. It also helped me process why my father may see laziness or being unproductive as negative actions. It has taken generations for us to understand rest as an act of resistance and self-preservation.

You deserve the nap, the trip, and the uninterrupted moment of stillness. You deserve to celebrate moments despite dealing with life's hardships. After all, there will always be some type of challenges to face, won't there? The greater the responsibilities we take on within our families and communities, the more essential it is to prioritize self-preservation.

Find Your Joy

When I was a little girl, I remember quietly closing my door to have a party for one in front of my mirror. Despite what was going on outside my bedroom door, despite the chaos, I would give myself a moment to rejoice in good vibrations. I still do that today, especially after a long trying day. When I recognize that I haven't made time for joy, I will find a mirror and dance or put on a song that lifts my spirits. This is how I break generational silence: through dance. Whether that was during my time as a professional dancer or by dancing at home, at social gatherings, or in my solitude. This choice of movement traces back way beyond my mother's ambitions for dance, honoring my ancestors and the cultures of the African diaspora, where dance was a crucial form of celebration and communication. Dance serves as my medium for storytelling when I can't find the words, and at times, it's the way in which I release the day's sorrows or stress.

Where do you find your joy in your current environment and situation? Is your expression of joy healthy for your mind, body, and spirit?

In my late twenties, I started to question if I really needed alcohol or substances to enjoy myself. Tired of the hangovers and the late nights spent partying with friends, I began experimenting with fasting as a way to test my strength and challenge some of my relationships. I wanted to evaluate whether any of my friendships or connections were rooted in unhealthy habits, including trauma bonding. When I say habits, I don't just mean alcohol or things I was putting into my body; I also wanted to fast from negative conversations that were judgmental or gossip-focused.

Cutting out unhealthy habits isn't easy. Some say it takes 21 days to one month to establish a new routine, but research from the *European Journal of Social Psychology* suggests the timeline can vary widely, from 18 to 254 days.[1] So if you've ever tried to break a habit and fell short after a few weeks, don't be so hard on yourself. There really is no one-size-fits-all approach to breaking our own habits, so as we work to find our rhythm, we must give ourselves grace. When testing what worked best for me, I found the most success when I set a sixty-day goal for my first fast and, in turn, decided to give up three things: alcohol, fried food, and speaking about others in a way I wouldn't feel comfortable doing to their face—all things I felt my mind and body could use a break from.

The first fast was so effective I extended it to ninety days and invited a friend to join me for the extension. After the completion of each week, I journaled to document my learnings and record the benefits for future reference. It was important for me to reflect on whether I felt any urge to revert to my previous habits. I chose to resume drinking occasionally but opted to continue abstaining from fried food a while longer. While the fast didn't lead to me completely abandoning these habits, it demonstrated the extent of my willpower and my ability to make healthier choices. From there, I made it a habit to partake in occasional fasts when I felt the need to take a break from something. Could you benefit from a fast? Is this a practice you've done for personal reasons, or were you inspired by generational religious traditions?

Being a Baptist, I choose to use fasting in a more personal and flexible way to correct negative behavioral traits and inspire personal growth. Fasting dates back centuries and plays a central role in many cultures and religions, often with more strictly enforced rules. For many, it serves as a means of spiritual reflection, purification, and discipline. In Islam, fasting is central to Ramadan, while Christianity adopts fasting during Lent. Judaism observes fasting on Yom Kippur for atonement, and both Buddhism and Hinduism use it for spiritual cleansing and meditation. Fasting across multiple religious groups and individuals is seen as a way to get closer to God and a healthier state of mind. So fast as needed.

As you intentionally center joy in your life, choose your company wisely. When my health declined in 2022, I decided to adopt an anti-inflammatory diet. I gave up hard liquor, dairy, red meat, and unhealthy oils. I tried to become more aware of what I was putting into my body and how it made me feel. Most of my family and friends supported my decision because it was a matter of life or death, but interestingly, some people encouraged me to cheat or break my fast for their own selfish gains. These were usually the individuals who either didn't understand my choice or chose to disregard the demands of their own bodies and well-being.

Communicating your needs is essential in building a circle of reliable friends and supporters who understand how to be there for you effectively. This support group is crucial for emotional and even physical well-being, providing understanding and encouragement to keep you on track. When you're someone who constantly looks after others, you also need people to look after you! Over time, I've been fortunate enough to cultivate a large support group, and I seize every opportunity to express my gratitude toward them. My health journey has taught me the invaluable lesson that people are under no obligation to show up for us. Yet, for those who consistently do, it's important to me that they feel their love and support will be reciprocated.

Do You Know What Your Support Language Is?

Asking for help can be difficult. Over the years, I've learned to reach out to loved ones when I'm in need, and I've even created a code word for "911" so they know when I need them urgently. I've also been intentional in expressing what my "support language" looks like so they don't have to guess. For example, when I was sick, I received countless bouquets of flowers, and I would watch as they bloomed and died so quickly. I went from appreciating them to feeling sadness as I watched them wilt. After I came out of the hospital, I didn't want to see or receive any more flowers, but I also didn't want to come off as rude or ungrateful. I reached out to loved ones during my recovery time and respectfully asked that if they wanted to send anything to please send food over flowers. I needed to eat, and my husband was exhausted from caring for me and performing the household duties. Food offered us ease. It provided the support that our loved ones intended to give.

Have you shared with your loved ones how they can best provide comfort, encouragement, or support during your busy seasons? We can't assume that people know what we need. Learning our support languages, similar to how we know our love language, is important for ensuring you get what you need out of your relationships, and verbalizing these needs also reveals those in your life who truly want to be in your corner through every season. Oftentimes, how we show up for others is how we want people to show up for us. And if someone shows up for you in a way that you need, meet them with the same type of energy.

Do you know what type of support your family members need from you? When we show up for our elders, we bring them joy! They know more than anyone that their time is growing shorter. And sometimes it's the simplest act, like spending quality time or making a phone call, that can turn their day around. Our elders, who have endured many days of sorrow and difficulty, sometimes rely on our check-ins and stories to give them life. Sometimes support is just showing them that we're thinking of them.

My parents have shown up for me countless times throughout my life. As they're aging, I often think about how the favor should be reciprocated. My father, who is in his midsixties, is more frequently confronted with deaths of friends, family members, and peers. His brother, my uncle Bubba, would often call him nightly, and I know he misses that. Coping with these significant losses requires support from others, and I try to check in more often, calling simply to see how his day is going. For my mother, I want her to know that I will always show up in physical form whenever she needs me. While she wasn't always physically there for me, she was there emotionally and always one phone call away. In return, I choose to show up in both ways. Even with her living so far away, I never want her to feel like that will keep me from jumping on a plane in her times of need.

I also find joy in honoring some of my family traditions. For me, cracking jokes at BBQs, cooking (healthy) southern meals, doing the Electric Slide, coming together to celebrate all of the kids' birthdays, or going to church like my grandmother and great-aunt would've wanted are ways I honor my loved ones. In carrying their traditions, I express my gratitude.

Improve Your Health Through Joy

> "Be thankful for what you have; you'll end up
> having more. If you concentrate on what you
> don't have, you will never, ever have enough."
>
> —Oprah Winfrey

If you feel as though you have nothing to celebrate, you may struggle to find joy, but this feeling can also manifest even in the moments when you have it all. If you're having trouble cultivating joy in your daily life and need some practical steps on improving your overall mental health, here are some simple practices I've picked up along my journey of meeting happy people:

- **WRITE A GRATITUDE NOTE TO A RANDOM PERSON:** One of my board members has a habit of writing one letter a month to someone in her world who has impacted her in a positive way, small or large. She writes the letters and then mails them to those people. It's a practice that has grounded her and strengthened her relationships.

- **PRAY OUT LOUD OR IN YOUR MIND:** Each day I speak or sing to God and name the things I'm grateful for. This habit has become so consistent that I find myself asking for less and thanking Him more.

- **MEDITATE ON A PERSON, PLACE, OR THING THAT HAS HAD A POSITIVE IMPACT ON YOU:** Sit with this thought, breathe through the positive thoughts that arise, and say thank you.

- **KEEP A GRATITUDE JOURNAL:** You don't have to write in it every day, but writing about your blessings can help you shift your mind to positive thoughts, especially when your day has been challenging.

- **END YOUR NIGHT BY NAMING YOUR FAVORITE PART OF THE DAY:** Each night when my husband Kelsei and I get in bed, even if we're both exhausted, we lean in and ask each other to name our favorite part of the day. It helps us go to bed on a positive note, and it also helps us remember ways we can contribute to each other's joy. Sometimes it might be the simplest things, like having our favorite snack, reconnecting with an old friend, engaging in moments of intimacy, or something someone said at work. Sharing these experiences with your partner helps prioritize similar moments and provides space for us to find a positive in what might've felt like a difficult day.

- **FOCUS ON YOUR BREATHING:** To breathe means you're alive. Sometimes when I'm feeling overwhelmed or tired, I close my eyes and say "Thank you" as I inhale and exhale, taking deep breaths in sixty-second intervals. It's a reset for my entire nervous system.

> "Gratitude is the ability to experience life as a gift.
> It liberates us from the prison of self-preoccupation."
>
> —John Ortberg

A 2021 study published by the University of New England, Australia, uncovered something pretty amazing: being grateful can seriously lower your chances of feeling depressed.[2] It turns out, focusing on what you're thankful for can make you feel more optimistic and satisfied with life, and it can even give you a boost in self-esteem. Those who make it a point to count their blessings don't just have personal benefits; they enjoy stronger friendships and relationships as well. Gratitude provides our brains with a practice that helps us handle tough times, keeping us rooted in the now.

Furthermore, research published in 2019 in the *Journal of Positive Psychology* underscores the physical health benefits of gratitude, finding that maintaining a gratitude journal can lead to a notable decrease in diastolic blood pressure—the pressure exerted by the heart between beats.[3] Engaging in grateful reflection, even without writing down your thoughts, contributes to your heart health by calming and regulating your breathing to synchronize with your heartbeat. So why not shift our focus to the good? Make yourself, and even your heart, a lot happier. Bring in joy with this simple mind shift.

When Miracle comes home from school or work, she loves to vent. Her routine might be pretty consistent too: she sets her bags down, washes her hands, and then comes to tell me what went wrong or recount the day's frustrations. And in those moments, I can feel the cycle repeating from my own parents who used to do the same. Initially I appreciated that she looked forward to sharing and felt comfortable laying down her baggage with me. Then I realized that taking off her negative weight was affecting my well-being. Consequently, I introduced some gentle shifts in our interactions. On certain days, I encourage her to take a pause and first ask her to share one highlight from her day, and on other days, when I simply can't process any additional negativity, I ask her, "Do you mind telling someone else today? I want to hear about your day, but I have a lot on my plate. Let's talk later." My aim is not to dismiss her feelings, but by doing this, I'm honoring my own and sensitively responding to hers in an honest way. She responds positively to both approaches.

Help Yourself First

In the end, finding my purpose, reconnecting with my religion, improving my financial situation, setting better boundaries with my family, and improving my communication skills to advocate for myself have put me on a path that reduces my overall stress levels. Feeling less stressed and bogged down, I walk out of the door each day with my face to the sun rather than in my phone or to the pavement. There's a lot to fix in the world, but it's not my job alone to do. The process of fixing the world we all occupy is our shared responsibility as humans. We all have to play our part, and no one person or leader should feel they need to carry the complete burden of a group of people.

Through his social platforms, motivational speaker and author Jesse Itzler encourages us to introduce one winning habit into our lives each quarter. A winning habit is a consistent behavior or routine that contributes to achieving success and desired outcomes in various aspects of life, including personal development, career, and relationships. These are positive practices that, when regularly performed, enhance productivity, boost well-being, foster personal growth, and help in reaching one's goals. Examples of winning habits include effective time management, increasing our daily water intake, engaging in regular physical activity, mindfully eating, continuously learning, or practicing gratitude.

At the start of 2023, I chose to drop the habit of creating a New Year's resolution, and I instead identified three personal winning habits I could implement to help me get closer to my goals. Making it a point to start each morning with one of these options, I wake up each day and choose one of my three *W*'s: writing, working out, or walking. Some days this means jotting down a quick journal entry or walking to my local cafe for a pressed juice. I don't set a time limit, so there's less of a chance I'll see the winning habit as an obligation or interference to a potentially busy day. Sometimes my winning habit can take ten minutes, while other days, I lock in for forty-five minutes. By choosing to intentionally start my day by committing to one of these winning habits, I set a positive tone for my day. Winning is all about consistency.

Questions for Yourself

We end here, on a good note, with your final reflection. I invite you to take a few moments to reflect on the following questions so you can attract more joy into your world.

- What practical winning habits can I add to my daily routine?

- What positive spaces and energy do I need to surround myself with more?

- Am I content with where I'm going in life? What can I do today and tomorrow to invest in my happiness?

- Am I promoting healthy habits for future generations?

Healer's Recap

- The work must include rest.

- Filter out negative thoughts by focusing on gratitude.

- You deserve joy. Try to be more present and cultivate positive moments with self or what and who is in front of you.

- Form winning habits and practice fasting to reach your goals faster and eliminate the practices and behaviors you're least proud of.

- Identify what your "support language" is and tell people how to show up for you.

- Don't let the pressures of breaking cycles rob you of the joy you should experience in the process.

Closing Thoughts

The idea of breaking anything has historically had a negative connotation, but we're changing that with the work we're doing here. Through my personal stories and reflections, I hope you've gained some insight into how you can continue this work beyond this book and create positive change for your family and generations to come. Of course, we must acknowledge that we won't break every cycle overnight, but we can start by making sure we no longer hide our thoughts, feelings, and experiences in silence.

I pray that your family experiences healthier outcomes, financial freedom, emotional healing, and stronger relationships despite the oppressive states they may be living in. I hope you are now better equipped to understand your family and their flaws, I hope you can forgive those who have wronged you, and above all, I hope you realize you have absolutely everything you need. Use the journey I've outlined in this book to affirm to yourself that you are a cycle breaker. Embrace new beginnings and know that new traditions don't need endorsement. Follow your calling, and remember you can practice gratitude by simply thanking those who gave you life.

Notes

Introduction

1. Sarah A. Font, Lawrence M. Berger, and Kristen S. Slack, "Examining Racial Disproportionality in Child Protective Services Case Decisions," *Child and Youth Services Review* 34, no. 11 (November 2012), ncbi.nlm.nih.gov/pmc/articles/PMC3439815/.
2. Heather Andrea Williams, *Help Me to Find My People: The African American Search for Family Lost in Slavery* (University of North Carolina Press, 2012).

Chapter One: Your Mother's Tears

1. Jessica Cerdeña, Luisa M. Rivera, and Judy M. Spak, "Intergenerational Trauma in Latinxs: A Scoping Review," *Social Science & Medicine* 270, (January 2021), pubmed.ncbi.nlm.nih.gov/33476987/.
2. Crystal Raypole, "Understanding Intergenerational Trauma and Its Effects," *Healthline*, April 20, 2022, healthline.com/health/mental-health/intergenerational-trauma.
3. Michelle Anthony, "The Social and Emotional Lives of 8- to 10-Year Olds," Scholastic, accessed August 1, 2024, scholastic.com/parents/family-life/social-emotional-learning/development-milestones/emotional-lives-8-10-year-olds.html.
4. Toni Morrison, *Beloved* (New York: Alfred A. Knopf, 1987), 88.

5. James Weldon Johnson, lyricist, and John Rosamond Johnson, composer, "Lift Every Voice and Sing" (1900).

6. "Why Does Suicidal Ideation Rise from Isolation?," *Pasadena Villa* (blog), May 6, 2022, pasadenavilla.com/resources/blog/why-does-suicidal-ideation-rise-from-isolation/.

7. Amy Murnan, "Can Emotions Be Trapped in the Body? What to Know," *Medical News Today*, August 21, 2023, medicalnewstoday.com/articles/emotions-trapped-in-the-body#symptoms.

8. Joel Nigg, "How ADHD Amplifies Emotions," *Additude*, June 29, 2023, additudemag.com/emotional-dysregulation-adhd-video/.

9. Tanya Peterson, "Thought Stopping: Techniques, Effectiveness, and Alternatives," *Choosing Therapy*, September 28, 2023, choosingtherapy.com/thought-stopping/.

10. CNN, "Angelou: 'No one of us can be free until everybody is . . .'" YouTube video, youtube.com/watch?v=UxkTd6BFL1o.

11. Hamid Ullah et al., "Intergenerational Trauma: A Silent Contributor to Mental Health Deterioration in Afghanistan," *Brain and Behavior* 13, no. 4 (April 2023), ncbi.nlm.nih.gov/pmc/articles/PMC10097044/.

12. Janet Taylor, MD (community psychiatrist), in discussion with author, October 2023.

13. Ana Adan, "Cognitive Performance and Dehydration," *Journal of the American College of Nutrition* 31, no. 2 (April 2012), pubmed.ncbi.nlm.nih.gov/22855911/.

14. Jill Rosen, "What Looks Like Substance Abuse Could Be Rational Self-Medication, Study Suggests," *Johns Hopkins University—Hub*, December 18, 2018, hub.jhu.edu/2018/12/18/heavy-drinking-self-medication/.

15. United Nations Office on Drugs and Crime, *World Drug Report 2018: Drugs and Age; Drugs and Associated Issues Among Young People and Older People*, June 2018, unodc.org/wdr2018/prelaunch/WDR18_Booklet_4_YOUTH.pdf.

16. Janet Taylor, MD, in discussion with author, October 2023.

Chapter Two: It's Genetic: Health Talks for Survival

1. "Women and Pain: Disparities in Experience and Treatment," *Harvard Health Blog, Harvard Health Publishing*, October 9, 2017, health.harvard.edu/blog/women-and-pain-disparities-in-experience-and-treatment-2017100912562.

2. Megan E. Deichen Hansen et al., "Racial Inequities in Emergency Department Wait Times for Pregnancy-Related Concerns," *Women's Health (London)* 18 (October 2022), ncbi.nlm.nih.gov/pmc/articles/PMC9623347/.

3. Thomas Gordon, *Leader Effectiveness Training: L.E.T.* (Revised) (New York: Penguin Books, 2001), 108–12.

4. CardioSmart News, "Endometriosis Increases Risk for Heart Disease in Young Women," CardioSmart—American College of Cardiology, April 23, 2016, cardiosmart.org/news/2016/4/endometriosis-increases-risk-for-heart-disease-in-young-women.

5. Anna Tubbs (author), in discussion with author, January 2023.

6. Adrian F. Ward, "The Neuroscience of Everybody's Favorite Topic," *Scientific American*, July 16, 2013, scientificamerican.com/article/the-neuroscience-of-everybody-favorite-topic-themselves/.

Chapter Three: Just Getting By

1. Kristin Broady, Mac McComas, and Amine Quazad, "An Analysis of Financial Institutions in Black-Majority Communities: Black Borrowers and Depositors Face Considerable Challenges in Accessing Banking Services," Brookings, November 2, 2021, brookings.edu/articles/an-analysis-of-financial-institutions-in-black-majority-communities-black-borrowers-and-depositors-face-considerable-challenges-in-accessing-banking-services/.

2. "Disparities," Indian Health Service, updated October 2019, ihs.gov/newsroom/factsheets/disparities/.

3. Ramsey, "Which States Require Financial Literacy for High School Students?" Ramsey Solutions, March 11, 2024, ramseysolutions.com/financial-literacy/states-require-financial-literacy-in-high-school.

4. Diana Isern (founder of Fin Lit Legacies and vice principal and financial literacy educator at Brooklyn Preparatory High School), in discussion with author, April 2024.
5. Diana Isern, in discussion with author.
6. Lynne Twist, *The Soul of Money: Transforming Your Relationship with Money and Life* (W. W. Norton & Company, 2017).
7. Cary Funk and Mark Hugo Lopez, "Hispanic Americans' Experiences with Health Care," in Hispanic Americans' Trust in and Engagement with Science (report), Pew Research Center, June 14, 2022, pewresearch.org/science/2022/06/14/hispanic -americans-experiences-with-health-care/.

Chapter Four: Limited Dreams and Aspirations

1. Andrew Howard Nicols and J. Oliver Schak, *Degree Attainment for Black Adults: National and State Trends* (The Education Trust, 2017), edtrust.org/wp-content/uploads/2014/09/Black-Degree -Attainment_FINAL.pdf.
2. Kendra Cherry, "Maslow's Hierarchy of Needs," *Verywell Mind*, April 2, 2024, verywellmind.com/what-is-maslows-hierarchy-of -needs-4136760.
3. "State of Global Workplace: 2023 Report," Gallup Workplace, accessed July 8, 2024, gallup.com/workplace/349484/state-of -the-global-workplace.aspx.
4. Devi Brown (author and multidisciplinary healer), in discussion with author, January 2024.

Chapter Five: Navigating Racism

1. Shadya Karawi-Name, "How to Heal Our Childhood's 5 Emotional Wounds," *Discovering Therapy* (blog), June 25, 2019, discoveringtherapy.com/blog/how-to-heal-our-childhood-s-5 -emotional-wounds/.
2. Karawi-Name, "How to Heal."
3. Devin English et al., "Daily Multidimensional Racial Discrimination Among Black U.S. American Adolescents,"

Journal of Applied Developmental Psychology 66, sciencedirect.com
/science/article/abs/pii/S0193397319300462; see also Annie
Ma, "Black Kids Face Racism Before They Even Start School.
It's Driving a Mental Health Crisis," *AP News*, May 23, 2023,
projects.apnews.com/features/2023/from-birth-to-death/mental
-health-black-children-investigation.html.

4. "Racism and Health," CDC, June 20, 2024, cdc.gov/minority
-health/racism-health/.

5. Rupa Marya and Raj Patel, *Inflamed: Deep Medicine and the Anatomy
of Injustice* (New York: Farrar, Straus, and Giroux, 2021).

6. *Slave Narratives : A Folk History of Slavery in the United States from
Interviews with Former Slaves*, vol. 14, South Carolina, Genealogy
Trails, genealogytrails.com/scar/hampton/slave_narratives.htm.

Chapter Six: Who Is God to You?

1. Neha Sahgal and Greg Smith, "A Religious Portrait of African-
Americans," Pew Research Center, January 30, 2009, pewresearch
.org/religion/2009/01/30/a-religious-portrait-of-african-americans/.

2. National Humanities Center Resource Toolbox, "Religious
Practice of Enslaved African Americans in the Southern
United States," *The Making of African American Identity* 1,
nationalhumanitiescenter.org/pds/maai/community/text3
/religionslaveswpa.pdf.

3. National Humanities Center Resource Toolbox, *The Making of
African American Identity* 1.

4. National Humanities Center Resource Toolbox.

5. Besheer Mohamed et al., "Faith Among Black Americans," Pew
Research Center, February 16, 2021, pewresearch.org/religion
/2021/02/16/faith-among-black-americans/.

Chapter Seven: Violence Epidemic

1. *Statistics about Sexual Violence* (National Sexual Violence Resource
Center, 2015), nsvrc.org/sites/default/files/publications_nsvrc
_factsheet_media-packet_statistics-about-sexual-violence_0.pdf.

Chapter Eight: Coping in Silence

1. Joshua Gibbs, "What Is the Difference Between Quiet and Silence?" *Circe Institute* (blog), August 30, 2016, circeinstitute.org/blog/blog-what-difference-between-quiet-and-silence/.

2. William Damon and Richard M. Lerner, eds., *Handbook of Child Psychology: Social, Emotional, and Personality Development*, 6th ed. (Hoboken, NJ: John Wiley & Sons, 2006).

Chapter Nine: Silent Apologies

1. "Psychotherapies," National Institute of Mental Health, February 2024, nimh.nih.gov/health/topics/psychotherapies.

2. Alexandra Roxo, *Dare to Feel: The Transformational Path of the Heart* (Sounds True, 2024).

3. Angela Haupt, "8 Ways to Apologize Well," *Time*, March 24, 2023, time.com/6264614/how-to-apologize-health-benefits/.

4. Suzanne Phillips, "What Makes an Apology Effective in Healing?" *Couples After Trauma*, October 10, 2016, couplesaftertrauma.com/2016/10/10/what-makes-an-apology-effective-in-healing/.

5. Rachel Wilkerson Miller, "How to Forgive Someone Who Isn't Sorry," *Vox*, March 25, 2022, vox.com/22967752/how-to-forgive-someone-who-isnt-sorry-wont-apologize.

6. Lisa Tams, "The Importance of Forgiveness," Michigan State University Extension, December 12, 2016, canr.msu.edu/news/the_importance_of_forgiveness.

7. "New York Lawmakers OK Bill to Consider Reparations for Slavery," CBS News, June 9, 2023, cbsnews.com/news/new-york-lawmakers-ok-bill-to-consider-reparations-for-slavery-historic/.

Chapter Ten: We Are Enough!

1. Geoffrey L. Cohen, "How the Need to Belong Drives Human Behavior" in Speaking of Psychology, podcast, apa.org/news/podcasts/speaking-of-psychology/human-behavior.

Chapter Eleven: Advocate for a Better World

1. "Black People More Than Three Times as Likely as White People to Be Killed During a Police Encounter," Harvard T.H. Chan School of Public Health, accessed June 24, 2024, hsph.harvard.edu/news /hsph-in-the-news/blacks-whites-police-deaths-disparity/.
2. "Homelessness," National Foster Youth Institute, 2015, nfyi.org /issues/homelessness/.
3. Joshua Rovner, "Black Disparities in Youth Incarceration," The Sentencing Project, December 12, 2023, sentencingproject.org/fact -sheet/black-disparities-in-youth-incarceration/#footnote-ref-5.
4. 1 Cor. 14:34.
5. Jarena Lee, "My Call to Preach the Gospel," Teaching American History, accessed August 2, 2024, teachingamericanhistory.org /document/my-call-to-preach-the-gospel/.

Chapter Twelve: Joy Out Loud

1. Phillippa Lally et al., "How Are Habits Formed: Modelling Habit Formation in the Real World," *European Journal of Social Psychology* 40, no. 6 (October 2010), onlinelibrary.wiley.com/doi /abs/10.1002/ejsp.674.
2. Jo A. Iodice, John M. Malouff, and Nicola S. Schutte, "The Association Between Gratitude and Depression: A Meta-Analysis," *International Journal of Depression and Anxiety* 4, no. 1 (June 2021), clinmedjournals.org/articles/ijda/international -journal-of-depression-and-anxiety-ijda-4-024.php.
3. Lilian Jans-Beken et al., "Gratitude and Health: An Updated Review," *Journal of Positive Psychology* 15, no. 6 (August 2019), doi.org/10.1080/17439760.2019.1651888.

About the Author

Nicole Russell-Wharton is a certified trauma-informed healing instructor. She is the founder and executive director of the Precious Dreams Foundation, a global non-profit organization that advocates for mental health and the well-being of children, and the owner of Restorative Commons, which promotes equity by way of rest and resources for advocates and community change-makers.

An accomplished author, her bestselling YA self-help book, *Everything a Band-Aid Can't Fix*, is a cornerstone resource for teens across the nation and is integrated into middle and high school curriculums. Inspired by her own journey with ADHD, her first children's book, *My Busy, Busy Brain*, encourages young readers to embrace their unique challenges and advocate for themselves.

Nicole's impactful work has earned her numerous accolades, including *Glamour*'s "Everyday Hero of the Year," *Observer*'s "Top 20 Heroes Under 40," and recognition in *O, The Oprah Magazine*. Most recently, she was honored by NBC and *Essence* for her tireless efforts to support the mental health needs of youth during the pandemic.

With unwavering empathy and bold leadership, Nicole Russell-Wharton is on a mission to teach the world how to nurture young people's voices, empowering them to advocate for their well-being and futures. She calls New York City home.

About Sounds True

Sounds True was founded in 1985 by Tami Simon with a clear mission: to disseminate spiritual wisdom. Since starting out as a project with one woman and her tape recorder, we have grown into a multimedia publishing company with a catalog of more than 3,000 titles by some of the leading teachers and visionaries of our time, and an ever-expanding family of beloved customers from across the world.

In more than three decades of evolution, Sounds True has maintained our focus on our overriding purpose and mission: to wake up the world. We offer books, audio programs, online learning experiences, and in-person events to support your personal growth and awakening, and to unlock our greatest human capacities to love and serve.

At SoundsTrue.com you'll find a wealth of resources to enrich your journey, including our weekly *Insights at the Edge* podcast, free downloads, and information about our nonprofit Sounds True Foundation, where we strive to remove financial barriers to the materials we publish through scholarships and donations worldwide.

To learn more, please visit SoundsTrue.com/freegifts or call us toll-free at 800.333.9185.

Together, we can wake up the world.

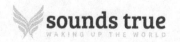